BUS

ACPL ITEM
DISCARDED

388.42 M58f
Middleton, William D., 1928-
From bullets to BART

D0923135

FROM BULLETS TO BART

BULLET 202 of the Philadelphia Suburban Transportation Company approached Bryn Mawr station on September 8, 1951. When these cars entered service in 1931 little did anyone realize that they would be still carrying people between Norristown and the 69th Street Terminal near Philadelphia in 1989. These cars are symbolic for many reasons. To CERA they are symbolic because they have served throughout the 50 year plus existence of CERA. *(WCJ)* BART (Bay Area Rapid Transit) began operations on September 11, 1972. On March 26, 1975, this Fremont train was approaching the MacArthur station in Oakland *(WDM)* BART is not the newest rapid transit system in the United States. However, BART is viewed by many observers as starting the new age of electric railroads in the United States. Both the Bullets and BART were innovations for their time. Together they represent the time when CERA began and when CERA celebrated its fiftieth anniversary.

FROM BULLETS TO BART

Bulletin 127 of the Central Electric Railfans' Association

WILLIAM D. MIDDLETON, AUTHOR

NORMAN CARLSON, EDITOR

Issued in commemoration of the Fiftieth
Anniversary of Central Electric Railfans' Association
1938-1988

FROM BULLETS TO BART

Bulletin 127 of the Central Electric Railfans' Association

Copyright 1989 by the Central Electric Railfans' Association
All rights reserved
An Illinois Not-for-Profit Corporation
Post Office Box 503, Chicago, Illinois 60690, U.S.A.

Library of Congress Catalog Card Number 88-070491
International Standard Book Number 0-915348-27-4

Allen County Public Library
900 Webster Street
PO Box 2270
Fort Wayne, IN 46801-2270

AUTHOR:
  WILLIAM D. MIDDLETON

EDITOR:
  NORMAN CARLSON

EDITORIAL STAFF:
  Roy G. Benedict   Raymond F. Corley   George Krambles
  James J. Buckley   William C. Janssen   Arthur H. Peterson

CERA DIRECTORS 1988-1989
  Norman Carlson   Frederick D. Lonnes   Charlie W. Petzold
  Phillip F. Cioffi   Donald L. MacCorquodale   William M. Shapotkin
  Walter R. Keevil   Bruce G. Moffat   Jeffrey L. Wien
                          Stanford A. Nettis

All rights reserved. No part of this book may be commercially reproduced or utilized in any form, except for brief quotations, nor by any means electronic or mechanical, including photocopying or recording, nor by any informational storage retrieval system, without permission in writing from the Central Electric Railfans' Association.

CERA Bulletins are technical, educational references prepared as historical projects by members of the Central Electric Railfans' Association, working without salary due to their interest in the subject. This Bulletin is consistent with this stated purpose of the corporation: To foster the study of the history, equipment and operation of electric railways. If you can provide additional information, or are of the opinion that any statement herein is inaccurate or incomplete, please send documentation supporting such amendment or correction, citing sources, to the Central Electric Railfans' Association, P.O. Box 503, Chicago, Illinois 60690, U.S.A.

FROM BULLETS TO BART (B-127) was designed by Norman Carlson. Color separations and assembly are by Jim Walter Graphics Arts of Beloit, Wisconsin with typesetting and printing by Sorg Printing Company of Illinois and binding by Zonne Bookbinders of Chicago, Illinois

CONTENTS:

PHOTOGRAPHERS:

This commemorative publication would not have been possible without the photographic contributions of the following people. Their willingness to share this excellent photography has made this book more memorable. In some cases we have merely identified by their initials, a tradition that was established in early CERA Bulletins. To long-time members the initials and the photographers are well remembered and friends to many. To our new members and readers we not only want to introduce them but to also recognize their significant contributions as well. Thank you does not seem to adequately convey our gratitude for their assistance. These principal contributors are:

George Krambles   (GK)
William C. Janssen   (WCJ)
Robert V. Mehlenbeck   (RVM)
William D. Middleton   (WDM)
Fred W. Schneider III (FWS)

Other members and friends who willingly dug into their vast collection, or whose work was contributed by other collectors, also deserve recognition. Their support is invaluable. These people are:

Roy G. Benedict
John J. Bowman, Jr.
Thomas H. Desnoyers
John Harder
Herbert H. Harwood, Jr.
John F. Humiston
Philip C. Johnson
Walter R. Keevil
Gordon E. Lloyd

To these gentlemen we say thank you very much for making this a truly noteworthy publication.

Baltimore Transit Company PCC 7030, posed shortly after its delivery in June 1939, was resplendent in its color scheme of Alexander Blue and cream with an orange belt rail and pearl gray roof *(General Electric photo, Krambles Collection)*

ACKNOWLEDGMENTS:

While a series of events were held over the 1988 Memorial Day weekend to commemorate the fiftieth anniversary of Central Electric Railfans' Association a more lasting commemorative seemed appropriate. The result is this book, *From Bullets to BART,* a fifty year history of the electric railway industry. A period in which we have seen the decline, nadir and rebirth of the industry. In both 1987 and 1988 over $1 Billion of railroad passenger rolling stock was delivered in the United States. The majority of that rolling stock with either electrically powered self-propelled cars or rolling stock pulled by electric locomotives. Electrifications were extended and significant improvements made in existing infrastructures. All of this investment is being made in railroads, an industry that many people think is dying. Those of us who study the industry have a different view.

CERA is extremely fortunate to be able to present a work by William D. Middleton. Bill is clearly the "dean" of the authors on electric traction. His published works include 400 articles for magazines and newspapers around the world and twelve books on railroads and electric traction. This is his first work for CERA and it is significant because in commemoration of our fiftieth anniversary Bill donated his work. Bill willingly accepted the invitation to document the history of this fifty year period. Not only did Bill author this text but he presented this material at a meeting in Chicago that was attended by over 525 people. The events of this golden anniversary celebration are described in a special supplement that begins on page 138 of CERA Bulletin 126, *A Rainbow of Traction.*

The value of this book is increased by the quality of the photographers whose contributions are separately acknowledged. We could not do this book without them. Captions of a quality necessary to support these extraordinary photographics was the final challenge. First to offer support was George Krambles whose assistance in the rapid transit chapter was significant. George as well as Roy Benedict, Jim Buckley, Ray Corley, Bill Janssen and Art Peterson assisted in the research. We also must recognize my secretary Marge Lester and Nancy Womack and all the other people in the typing and proofreading section of Arthur Andersen & Co. in Chicago who waded through the editor's handwriting to create a product worthy of typesetting by the people at Sorg Printing. The efforts of all of these people is much appreciated.

CERA is blessed with a fine production crew. Jim Walter always goes beyond the call of duty to assist in any way he can. For almost 15 years Jim has been working on our books, always advancing the quality of reproduction of the historic photos that we present. Wally Maier and Ann O'Brien at Sorg Printing continually offer suggestions and work hard to improve the quality of our books. Bob Goodman at Zonne Bookbinders always makes suggestions to improve the binding and tends to many details that result in the finished product that you receive. We should also recognize CERA's Board of Directors as they approved and authorized this project. Finally we must say thanks to Mary Carlson for her support and encouragement in letting her husband "do his thing" even though it meant even more time away from her.

While we have already mentioned George Krambles we should give him special recognition. George is one of the founders of CERA and in many respects is *the* reason that CERA exists today. How many international organizations can say that 51 years later their founder is active and making significant contributions to the organization? George is CERA member number 1. Two other of the significant contributors to this book are Bill Jenssen and Bob Mehlenbeck, members 10 and 11 respectively. Long time contributions by these and other gentlemen is the strength of CERA.

To all of you we say thank you, thank you very much.

Norman Carlson

Chicago, Illinois
July, 1989

AUTHOR'S PREFACE

One of the special fascinations of electric railways is that their enthusiasts can approach the subject from such a wide range of viewpoints. For the antiquarian, electric traction is a century-old industry rich in history and nostalgia. For the futurist, electric railways represent a contemporary technology that is assuming a growing importance in helping to make the world's modern cities into more livable places. For me, and I suspect for much of the C.E.R.A. membership, both of these views of electric traction are relevant. In fact, I would maintain that it is this very combination of a varied and colorful history with an enduring and continuing vitality and utility in the modern world that gives electric railways their enormous appeal for so many of us.

The task of reviewing the electric railway's evolution over the C.E.R.A.'s first half century turned out to be quite an assignment indeed, for what an extraordinary fifty years it was for electric traction in all its diversity of forms.

In the C.E.R.A. half century we've seen the street railway go from Depression decline to the P.C.C. revolution, to decline again, and then to the streetcar's modern light rail renaissance. Despite *Electroliners*, C.A.&E. 450's, or Illinois Terminal streamliners we saw the interurbans all but vanish. But two survivors endured in Indiana and Pennsylvania to remind us of what had been, and to show us, in the form of South Shore's magnificent stainless steel third generation interurbans from Japan or SEPTA's P&W Bullet replacements now abuilding in Sweden, what an interurban future could have been like. Indeed, as the half century neared its end there were even new light rail projects under construction or planned that were putting electric traction back in some of the interurban corridors of old.

For main line electrification it was mostly a half century of decline, but it was a time, too, for the glory years of Pennsy GG1's; for *Metroliners* and A.S.E.A. AEM1's at 120 m.p.h. on a superbly modernized Northeast Corridor; for *Metropolitan, Cosmopolitan,* and *Jersey Arrow* commuting; or for 25 and 50 KV heavy freight haulers beginning to appear under the catenary of new U.S. coal roads, and in the Canadian Rockies and Mexico.

Only for North American rapid transit was it a half century of unabashed growth. The "first generation" rapid transit systems at Boston, New York, Philadelphia, and Chicago all grew and modernized. New systems opened or began construction in a dozen conurbations as diverse as Montreal, Vancouver, Miami, Los Angeles, and Mexico City, utilizing computers, electronics, and new materials technologies to provide a highly sophisticated, and heavily automated "new generation" of rapid transit systems.

Beginning in the uncertainty of a fading Depression, the first C.E.R.A. half century ends at a time of extraordinary promise for the future of electric traction. Surely C.E.R.A.'s second fifty years will prove to be every bit as eventful as the first fifty.

When Norman Carlson extended an invitation to write the text for this review of electric traction during C.E.R.A.'s first half century, it was an assignment accepted with real enthusiasm. For all the reasons I've noted above, it was an uncommonly interesting period to write about. But equally important, it was a welcome opportunity to contribute to the commemoration of an important milestone in the history of an organization that has meant much to me, and to anyone with an interest in knowing and understanding electric traction in North America. Over its first half century C.E.R.A. has faithfully recorded the history of America's electric railways in a series of publications of extraordinary depth and quality that represent one of the most impressive records of rail history publication achieved by any organized enthusiast group, and a body of reference work of inestimable value. In appreciation for all that the Association has meant to all of us, I salute C.E.R.A. on the completion of its first half a century, and look forward to the second.

—William D. Middleton

Charlottesville, Virginia
May 1989

7

CHAPTER 1

FROM PCC TO LRV: FIFTY YEARS OF STREETCARS

Throughout the 1930's there wasn't much to feel good about in the street railway industry. By most measures the industry had hit its peak around the end of World War I. After that, beset by rising costs and the growing popularity of the automobile and the motor bus, the streetcar had entered a gradual decline. Trolley ridership had begun to fall by the early 1920's, and after 1922 the transit industry's operating revenues began a steady decline. By 1922, some 18 percent of the industry was in receivership.

The Great Depression that began late in 1929 only made matters worse. Trolley ridership, which had totaled some 10.5 billion annual passengers as recently as 1930, had dropped to just over 6.5 billion by 1938. Streetcar track miles were declining almost as rapidly as trolley lines were converted to bus operation; from 1930 to 1938 urban street railway mileage in the U.S. dropped from some 23,900 track miles to only 15,900, a decline of more than a third.

But by the late 1930's there was some good news for streetcar partisans, too, and that was the PCC car. The PCC was a product of efforts begun by the industry in the 1920's to produce an improved streetcar that could compete more effectively with private automobiles through enhanced efficiency, performance and comfort. Alloy steels and aluminum had been used to produce extremely light-weight cars. New motor and control designs had improved performance characteristics, while new trucks incorporated such advances as roller bearings, rubber cushioning, and automotive type gear drives to reduce noise and improve riding qualities. Such features as individual leather upholstered seats and rubber-tiled floors improved passenger comfort, while more modern lines and appealing color schemes helped to improve streetcar appearance.

These individual efforts to develop a better car met with some success, and significant numbers of standardized modern cars were built by several builders during the late 1920's. But much more than these modest improvements were needed to make the streetcar truly competitive, and it was an extraordinary industry-wide joint effort launched in 1929 that was to produce the revolutionary PCC streetcar. Organized by more than 50 operating companies and manufacturers, the Electric Railway Presidents' Conference Committee spent close to a million dollars in a five-year research and development program to produce a new standardized streetcar of radically improved appearance and performance. The new PCC incorporated such features as a streamlined carbody of welded high-tensile steel that weighed far less than any previous car of comparable size. Comfortably cushioned seating and improved heating, lighting, and ventilating systems contributed to greater passenger comfort. Remarkably quiet operation was achieved through extensive use of rubber insulation and rubber-cushioned wheels in the entirely new PCC truck design. Newly developed traction motors gave the PCC the highest power-to-weight ratio in streetcar history, with corresponding improvements in acceleration and operating speed. Equally improved braking performance was achieved through the use of dynamic braking, supplemented by magnetic track brakes and air brakes.

Following the development of an experimental unit, the Model "B" PCC car, in 1934, the first production PCC car had appeared in May 1936 when the first of a 100-car order was delivered by St. Louis Car Company to the Brooklyn & Queens Transit Corporation. The new car was a phenomenal success. Soon after the first PCCs went into service, streetcar companies were reporting ridership increases of anywhere from 5 to 15 percent; on one Brooklyn PCC line, traffic increased by 33 percent. Most PCC operators were able to increase schedule speeds by 10 percent or more, with several lines achieving speed gains of as much as 15 percent. Accident rates were reduced by as much as 30 percent. PCC cars consumed less power than the older cars they replaced, and maintenance costs were reduced; in Washington, D.C., PCC maintenance costs of 1.56 cents per car mile were little more than half those for the system's conventional streetcar equipment.

By the end of 1936 more than 200 PCC cars had gone into operation at Brooklyn, Chicago, and Baltimore, and within another two years almost 800 of the streamlined cars were in service in almost a dozen U.S. and Canadian cities. By the end of 1940 North American PCC ownership totaled more than 1200 cars.

But for all the success of the new PCC cars wherever they were introduced, the overall decline of the electric street railway in North America continued. By 1940 annual streetcar ridership had fallen to less than 6 billion passengers, and the industry's annual streetcar operating revenues of $299 million were scarcely half of what they had been only a decade previous. Streetcar track mileage continued to decline, while motor bus operations grew correspondingly.

For a few brief years, however, the streetcar's decline was reversed by the unprecedented economic activity—and the automobile and gasoline shortages—of the World War II years. PCC car production continued at a record level all through the war years; from 1941 through 1945 more than 1500 cars were produced for U.S. and Canadian lines. At the same time, fleets of older streetcars were overhauled to help transport a level of streetcar ridership that hadn't been seen since the end of the 1920s. By 1944 streetcar traffic had reached a wartime peak of more than 9.5 billion riders, an increase of 60 percent above the 1940 level. Except for a few marginal lines, street railway abandonments were virtually discontinued for the duration of the war.

For many of the large streetcar companies, this wartime traffic resurgence inspired what was to prove an unwarranted optimism about the future of the street railway. PCC car production surged to record levels in the years immediately after the end of the war in 1945, as some 18 U.S. and Canadian cities either ordered their first PCCs or expanded their streamliner fleets. More than 500 PCCs were delivered in 1946. Almost 700 of the new cars were placed in service in 1947, and production the following year was well over 600 cars. Before the end of the decade Chicago and Pittsburgh, the two largest PCC operators, each owned fleets of nearly 700 PCCs. Washington, Toronto, and Philadelphia each operated fleets of nearly 500 cars. St. Louis owned 300 PCCs, and Baltimore and Boston each operated almost as many. By the time domestic PCC production ended with a 25-car order delivered to San Francisco in 1952, over 4900 PCCs had been built for North American cities.

Well before World War II the superiority of the motor bus for lightly patronized transit routes had already been well established. Before the end of the 1930's busses had largely replaced streetcars in smaller American cities, and even in the larger cities busses had displaced the electric cars from many of the less heavily traveled routes. But well through the 1940's there were still those in the transit industry who considered the streetcar to be the superior mode for the most heavily traveled urban transit routes. The cars were capable of handling much heavier passenger loads than busses, with a correspondingly lower "platform" cost per rider, and the sizable fixed costs for streetcar track and electrical system maintenance could be spread over a greater number of passengers. It was for routes like these that the PCC car had the greatest advantage. The improved passenger appeal, greater productivity, and lower operating costs of the new cars, compared to older conventional equipment, simply enhanced the overall advantages of the streetcar for heavy urban transit lines.

World War II, as it turned out, was to prove the last stand of the streetcar, in its traditional form at least, as a major force in North American urban transportation. For despite the significant introduction of new PCC cars, street railway ridership resumed a rapid descent as new automobiles and gasoline again became plentiful at war's end. In the five years after the war, streetcar ridership fell an average of more than 10 percent a year. By 1949, annual trolley passengers had dropped well below the lowest level of the depression years, and by 1950 the number had fallen to only 3.9 billion, scarcely 40 percent of the wartime peak of 1944.

Aside from what proved to be the last few orders for PCC cars, there just wasn't any encouraging news for the streetcar industry from the late 1940's onward. Virtually all of the small city streetcar system had closed before the war. Faced with both declining traffic and a need for major capital investments to replace obsolete rolling stock and to rebuild their worn out permanent way and power systems, transit systems in even the larger cities began to abandon their rail operations in favor of busses after the end of the war.

Tampa, Chattanooga, Newport News, Worcester, and Peoria were all among the cities that lost their streetcars in 1946. Louisville, Knoxville, Memphis, and Oklahoma City became "all bus" cities a year later. Phoenix, Omaha, the Key System local lines in Oakland and Berkeley, Wheeling (W. Va.), and Norfolk closed down in 1948, while Atlanta, Richmond, and San Diego followed in 1949. Portland (Ore.) and Denver closed their last trolley lines in 1950.

Through 1950 virtually all of the systems that ended streetcar operations were ones that had either been unable—or unwilling—to make the major investment in modern PCC cars and rehabilitation of their physical plant that was needed to continue a satisfactory streetcar service. In many cities, too, the streetcar had come to be thought of as old fashioned and outmoded, and the operating companies had been encouraged, or even forced, to discontinue trolley operation. In New York City, for example, Mayor Fiorello La Guardia's administration had pressured the Third Avenue Railway System into a 1940 agreement to give up its streetcar operations that brought a swift end to a modernization program with home-built lightweight cars. World War II delayed the rail abandonments, but Third Avenue lines on Manhattan were closed in 1946. Lines in the Bronx followed in 1948, in Mt. Vernon in 1950, and in Yonkers in 1952.

Even a few companies that had bought PCC cars had second thoughts about the future of streetcars as transit ridership began its rapid descent immediately after the war. The Louisville Railway Company, for example, had ordered 25 new PCCs from St. Louis Car early in 1945. The company soon had a change in heart, and the cars were exchanged with the Cleveland Transit System for busses and cash in 1946 before PCCs had carried so much as a single Louisville revenue passenger. The city's streetcar system shut down the following year. A particularly disappointing street railway abandonment in the immediate post-war years was that of the San Diego system in 1949, for the San Diego Electric Railway had been one of the earliest companies to order the newly-developed PCC car in 1936.

But San Diego proved to be only the first of the PCC-modernized systems to close as ridership continued to decline. Cincinnati, which had a fleet of more than 50 PCCs, discontinued streetcar operation in 1951. Birmingham and Cleveland, which together operated a hundred PCCs, followed suit the next year. The Twin City Rapid Transit Company and Detroit's Department of Street Railways, which owned PCC fleets totaling well over 300 cars, shut down streetcar operation abruptly in 1954 and 1956, only a few years after the majority of their new cars had been delivered. Atlantic City, which had modernized in the late 1930s with 25 streamlined Brilliners, ended street railway operation in 1955. Brooklyn, which had bought the very first production PCCs in 1936, and Vancouver, B.C., which had a 36-car PCC fleet, both closed down streetcar operations in 1956. Rochester (N.Y.) shut down its novel trolley subway, built in the bed of the old Erie Canal, the same year.

In many cities, traffic congestion had become so severe that the high performance PCC cars proved simply unable to achieve their full earning potential. Chicago, with a 683-car PCC fleet, was one of these. As early as 1953 the Chicago Transit Authority had concluded that streetcar operations were so badly impaired by heavy traffic that continued trolley operation was simply uneconomic. Over the next few years almost 600 of the newest CTA PCCs were scrapped and their major components incorporated into new PCC type rapid transit cars for the city's "L" and subway system. All Chicago streetcar operation ended in 1958.

Milwaukee, one of the few cities still operating streetcars that had never modernized its system, also closed its last trolley line in 1958, while Montreal, Dallas, and Ottawa all shut down their trolley systems the following year. Johnstown (Pa.), the smallest city to operate PCCs, closed down in 1960. Baltimore and Los Angeles, both major PCC car operators, ended trolley operations in 1963. St. Louis proved to be the last major North American city to give up street railway operation, when its Hodiamont line closed in 1966.

The dimensions of the streetcar's decline in the post-war years are perhaps best reflected by a few statistics. Street railway track mileage, which totaled some 16,480 track miles in 1945, had dropped to less than 10,000 miles by 1950, and below 1,000 by 1963. By the end of the 1960s, when there were less than 800 miles of street railway track still in operation, only some 4 percent of the 1945 U.S.

trolley network remained. Ridership fared even more badly. In 1945 streetcar passengers had totaled more than 9.4 billion. More than half this traffic was gone by 1950, and by 1955 little more than 10 percent remained. By 1960, streetcar passengers numbered only some 4 percent of the 1945 level, and by 1970 the annual trolley ridership of 235 million represented only 2 percent of the immediate post-war volume.

By the late 1960's, then, there seemed to be very few grounds for any kind of optimism about the future of the electric street railway in North America. It seemed fair to say that the industry was dead, or very nearly so.

But the low estate of the late 1960s was to prove the nadir of the fortunes of the North American streetcar. There would be a few more abandonments over the next decade or so. Cut off from its international route to Ciudad Juarez, Mexico, the El Paso trolley line was shut down in 1974. The rickety system at Veracruz, Mexico, closed in 1975, while the PCC-equipped system at Tampico operated through 1981. But aside from the failure of these few marginal operations, the balance of the streetcar survivors would endure, and even prosper.

Altogether, there would be nine surviving trolley systems in North America, at Boston, Newark, Philadelphia, Pittsburgh, Cleveland, New Orleans, San Francisco, Toronto, and Mexico City. Population densities and a strong pattern of transit utilization in the urban areas they served had much to do with the longevity of these remaining surface rail lines, but almost without exception the surviving systems also enjoyed some exceptional operating characteristics that gave them decided advantages over motor bus systems operating in public streets.

To an appreciable degree, each of these survivors enjoyed at least some of the characteristics of what was called, for a time, the "limited tramline" concept. More recently known as "light rail," the concept represented a form of electric railway operation that fell somewhere between a conventional streetcar operation in public thoroughfares and fully grade-separated "heavy rail" rapid transit. Light rail typically operated in some form of private right-of-way, reserved median, or even subway to avoid the restrictions of mixed operation with motor vehicle traffic. Even where operation in streets was necessary, the electric cars were often separated from other traffic. Grade crossings, rather than costly grade separations, were typically provided. Freedom from the constraints of street traffic, as well as a wider spacing of stations, permitted light rail systems to operate at higher overall speeds. The use of larger vehicles, and sometimes multiple unit control, helped to increase the carrying capacity of light rail systems above the usual level for ordinary streetcar lines.

At Boston, an extensive Green Line light rail network into the city's southwest suburbs combined reserved center median or private right-of-way operation on its outer sections with a long streetcar subway into congested downtown Boston. The oldest portion of the subway, opened in 1897, was America's first subway. The most recent portion of the Boston system was a long route to suburban Riverside, which opened in 1959 over an abandoned Boston & Albany commuter route.

In New Jersey, the Newark City Subway afforded a textbook example of the light rail concept. Constructed in the bed of the abandoned Morris Canal in 1935, the 4.3-mile Newark line operated entirely in subway or private right-of-way, linking Penn Station in downtown Newark with areas of the city to the west and north. Originally, several connecting streetcar lines operated into the city center via the subway. After these lines were abandoned, the subway was linked with a number of connecting bus routes.

A substantial part of Philadelphia's surviving streetcar system was made up of a network of West Philadelphia surface routes which reached the downtown area through a 2.5-mile tunnel between West Philadelphia and City Hall. The earliest portion of the subway dated to 1905. The remainder of Philadelphia's surviving streetcar system was made up of more conventional surface streetcar lines in North Philadelphia.

At Pittsburgh, trolleys had to operate through congested urban streets in the downtown "Golden Triangle" area, but the 3500-foot Mt. Washington trolley tunnel and extensive private right-of-way south of the downtown area gave the surviving South Hills trolley routes decided operating advantages over motor busses operating on the area's congested road system.

Cleveland's Shaker Heights Rapid Transit system represented one of the earliest—and best—examples of the kind of electric railway operation envisioned by the light rail concept. The Shaker Heights system had been a key element in the 1920's promotion of the exclusive new residential community being developed at Shaker Heights by Cleveland's noted real estate and railroad entrepreneurs, the brothers Oris P. and Mantis J. Van Sweringen. Opened in 1920, the Shaker Heights system substantially reached its full development in 1930 with completion of the new Cleveland Union Terminal, another Van Sweringen project. Between a subway terminal under the CUT terminal tower and Shaker Square, the line operated over a grade-separated rapid transit right-of-way. Beyond Shaker Square, separate SHRT lines operated in reserved center median track in Shaker and Van Aken boulevards.

At San Francisco, five surviving Municipal Railway streetcar lines gained many of the operating advantages of the light rail concept from the availability of two long streetcar tunnels and extensive center median or private right-of-way, although they entered the downtown area over street trackage in busy Market Street. Streetcars on a single remaining line at New Orleans, on St. Charles Avenue, operated largely free of street traffic constraints in a reserved center median. Mexico City's surviving trolley lines, too, enjoyed the advantages of traffic-free operation in center medians.

Toronto, alone among North American cities, continued to operate a conventional streetcar system located almost entirely in paved urban streets. From about the mid-1950's onward, the Toronto system ranked as the largest streetcar operation anywhere in North America. Widely regarded as one of the best transit systems in North America, the Toronto Transit Commission had pragmatically utilized the most advantageous transit mode, whether motor bus, trolley bus, streetcar, or—after 1954—rail rapid transit, to best meet the traffic needs of a given route. An unusually high level of ridership, too, had helped to preserve a strong Toronto streetcar system.

While their special operating conditions and physical characteristics played a large part in the retention of these last streetcar systems, the superior performance and passenger appeal of the PCC car was a major contributor to their survival as well. Boston, Philadelphia, Pittsburgh, San Francisco, and Toronto all began acquiring new PCCs before World War II, and continued to expand their fleets after the war. Cleveland's Shaker Heights Rapid Transit ordered its first PCCs soon after the war. By the time its last new PCC was delivered in 1949, the Pittsburgh Railways had acquired some 666 cars, one of the largest of all PCC fleets. Toronto bought some 540 new PCCs between 1938 and 1951, while Philadelphia's roster of new PCCs totaled nearly 500 and Boston acquired well over 300 new PCCs.

As some of the major PCC-equipped street railway properties began to abandon their rail operations in the 1950s, a number of the surviving systems were able to enlarge their PCC fleets with second hand equipment. Toronto expanded its PCC roster to the largest in North America with more than 200 cars originally built for Louisville, Cleveland, Birmingham, and Kansas City. Philadelphia acquired a total of 120 used PCCs from St. Louis and Kansas City. The Shaker Heights line acquired used cars from the Twin Cities and St. Louis, while additional St. Louis cars went to San Francisco. Dallas's 25-car fleet of double-ended PCCs went to Boston.

Two systems acquired their entire PCC car fleets on the used equipment market. The Newark City Subway was completely reequipped in 1953 with 30 surplus Twin City Rapid Transit cars. And except for a single sample PCC acquired in 1947, Mexico City was able to build a 275-car PCC fleet entirely with used cars from the Twin Cities and Detroit.

During the 1970's there was even a small market in "third hand" PCCs. As some of its streetcar routes were displaced by new rail rapid transit lines, Toronto sold some 59 PCCs for further service in the U.S. and Mexico that had originally come to TTC as used equipment. Philadelphia acquired former Birmingham and Kansas City cars from TTC, while some ex-Kansas City cars also went to San Francisco and Tampico. A batch of Toronto PCCs originally built for Cleveland "went home," so to speak, for further service on the city's Shaker Heights line. The latter system also acquired a pair of former Twin City Rapid Transit PCCs that had spent most of their service life on the Newark City Subway.

At New Orleans, the unique St. Charles streetcar line was bypassed by the modern PCC car, and a fleet of durable Perley A. Thomas standard streetcars of 1923-24 origin continued to operate the line, making it the last conventional streetcar service in North America. The line gained a place on the National Register of Historic Places in 1973, and managed to establish itself as a distinctive feature of the Crescent City much as the celebrated cable cars had become a unique symbol of San Francisco.

By the 1970s, there was a growing urgency for major rehabilitation of all of these aging streetcar systems. Track and structures, signalling, and power supply installations typically ranged upwards from a half century in age, while PCC car fleets dated from the late 1940's, or even earlier.

Generally, the big city transit systems had moved from private to public ownership during the 1950's and 1960's, as urban mass transportation became increasingly uneconomic. This shift in ownership meant that public funds were now available to help offset both capital and operating costs that could no longer be met from the fare box. Passage of the Urban Mass Transportation Act of 1964 provided a basis for federal funding of capital investments for transit, and—later—operating cost subsidies. It was these resources that established a basis for extensive rehabilitation and modernization of the surviving U.S. streetcar systems.

Fixed plant rehabilitation typically followed similar standards. Track was rebuilt with heavier, continuously welded rail, and new ballast and ties. Stations and other structures were rehabilitated and modernized, or replaced. New or improved train control and signalling systems were installed. Power supply systems were enlarged and modernized to handle heavier traffic, and overhead distribution systems were rebuilt.

In addition to extensive rehabilitation of their existing plant, two of these surviving systems were able to carry out major additions and improvements as well.

At San Francisco, the 1962 bond issue that made the Bay Area Rapid Transit (BART) system possible also included provision for a 3.2-mile Market Street transit subway for the San Francisco Municipal Railway, which gave all five of Muni's surviving streetcar lines a fast route to the Embarcadero. All five of San Francisco's "Muni Metro" rail lines were operating through the new subway by 1981.

At Pittsburgh, a Stage 1 light rail project completed early in 1987 provided a virtually new modern light rail system in place of one of the principal routes in the city's surviving South Hills trolley system. Within the downtown Golden Triangle, street trackage was replaced by a new 1.1-mile, three-station subway, part of it utilizing an old Pennsylvania Railroad tunnel. The rehabilitated, former Pennsylvania Railroad Panhandle Bridge provided a new route across the Monongahela River, linking the new subway with the old Mt. Washington tunnel and the South Hills trolley routes. South of the tunnel, the existing trolley route via Mt. Lebanon was entirely rebuilt to modern, double-track light rail standards. Between Dormont and Mt. Lebanon, twin 3,000-foot tunnels were driven near Washington Road to provide a new, traffic-free route through the Mt. Lebanon business district.

Several of the existing systems had plans for the development of new light rail lines as well. At Boston, the Massachusetts Bay Transportation Authority (MBTA) was considering new Green Line light rail routes to Dudley Square and West Medford. In addition to plans for a Stage 2 light rail modernization of the remainder of it existing South Hills trolley system, Pittsburgh's Port Authority Transit (PAT) was studying a proposed Spine Line Corridor light rail project that would extend from downtown Pittsburgh across the Allegheny River into the North Side area of the city, and east to Oakland and Squirrel Hill.

At San Francisco, the Municipal Railway had plans for an extension of its Muni Metro J Line to Balboa Park, and new lines along the Embarcadero to the China Basin and Fisherman's Wharf areas. Long-range plans contemplated new Muni light rail lines in heavily-traveled corridors in Geary Street and in Third Street to Hunter's Point. At Mexico City a rehabilitation project that is currently upgrading the city's remaining trolley lines to modern light rail standards will also include two new rail lines. At Toronto, work began in 1987 on a new Harbourfront light rail line.

By the mid-1970's there was increasing interest in the

development of entirely new light rail systems to help solve the urban transportation problems of North American cities. Strictly speaking, the first entirely new light rail system had opened in 1963, when Leonard's, a Fort Worth department store, completed a short subway-surface trolley line linking the company's downtown store with a nearby parking lot.

Surprisingly, perhaps, the first important new systems were completed by two cities in Canada's western province of Alberta. The first of these to open was a 4.5-mile line at Edmonton that operated from downtown to the city's northeastern section over a line installed in a Canadian National right-of-way. A 1.5-mile subway carried the line through downtown Edmonton. Subsequent additions have extended the line to a length of 6.4 miles, with a 1.5-mile extension across the Saskatchewan River to South Edmonton under construction, with a 1992 opening planned. In 1981, Calgary opened the first section of a new light rail system that has since grown to some 17 miles of line, with routes from downtown Calgary to the south, northeast, and northwest. Trains operate through the city center in a downtown transitway, and in reserved rights-of-way elsewhere.

The first new U.S. light rail system opened in 1981 at San Diego, where the regional Metropolitan Transit Development Board (MTDB) completed its 16-mile South Line between downtown San Diego and the Mexican border at San Ysidro. Trains operated through downtown San Diego streets and in the right-of-way of the former San Diego & Arizona Eastern Railroad. Construction began in 1984 for a planned 17-mile East Urban Line that would extend over an SD&AE branch to El Cajon. An initial 4.5-mile section opened to Euclid Avenue in 1986, with the full line scheduled for opening by 1989. Construction began early in 1988 for a third MTDB light rail route, the Bayside Line serving the downtown waterfront and convention center area. Still other proposed lines could eventually expand MTDB's light rail network to a regional system of well over a hundred miles, with routes extending to Santee, Del Mar and Oceanside, Pt. Loma, and Escondido.

A second new U.S. light rail system opened in 1984 at Buffalo, where the Niagara Frontier Transportation Authority (NFTA)

completed the first section of a 6.5-mile line from downtown Buffalo north to the South Campus of the State University of New York at Buffalo. Called "light rail rapid transit," the line incorporated elements of both typical light rail practice and those of a full rapid transit system. In the downtown area the line operated in typical light rail fashion, in a Main Street transit mall; elsewhere, the line was in subway, with full automatic train control, typical subway speeds, and high-level station platforms. NFTA had planned its light rail line as the initial core of what could eventually become a regional rail system. Extensions to Amherst and Tonawanda were the most likely to come next.

In September 1986 the Tri-County Metropolitan Transportation District of Oregon opened its 15-mile Banfield light rail line at Portland. Built as an alternative to cancelled freeways, the heart of the Banfield project was a rebuilding program for a section of the Banfield freeway that provided a light rail entrance to downtown Portland from east Multnomah County. At its outer end the line was built in the center median of Burnside Street and then joined a former Portland Traction interurban right-of-way to reach its Gresham terminal. Downtown Portland tracks were laid in city streets. A projected second Portland light rail route would operate west from the downtown area to Beaverton. Other proposed routes would extend north to Vancouver (Wash.), south to Oregon City, and to Southwest Portland.

Two entirely new California light rail systems opened in 1987.

"Overnight, Sacramento feels more like a major city," commented the *Sacramento Bee* after the first section of the Regional Transit District's 18.3-mile RT Metro opened in March. The balance of the system went into operation six months later.

Constructed, like the Portland system, largely with funds from cancelled freeway projects, the Sacramento light rail system was installed in unused freeway right-of-way, railroad rights-of-way, and city streets. A new K Street transit mall carried light rail trains through downtown Sacramento. The C-shaped system had routes radiating northeast from downtown Sacramento to the intersection of Watt Avenue and Interstate 80, and eastward along Folsom Avenue to Butterfield. Projected additions to the system included extensions of the two initial lines to Roseville and Folsom, while new routes would extend south from the city center and northwest to the Sacramento Airport.

In December the Santa Clara County Transportation Agency opened an initial north end section of its Guadalupe Corridor light rail system, with a second segment through downtown San Jose scheduled for a late spring, 1988 opening. When the full 19.2-mile system is operating in 1991, Santa Clara County's light rail trains will link the residential areas south of San Jose with the "Silicon Valley" high tech industrial parks of North San Jose and Santa Clara. South of San Jose the line is being built in a joint light rail/expressway right-of-way that was originally acquired for highway construction. Trains will operate through downtown San Jose in city streets and a new, five block transit mall. North of the downtown area light rail trains operate in center medians in North First Street and Tasman Drive to their Santa Clara terminal.

Santa Clara County transportation planners have identified at least four potential branches or extensions from the initial Guadalupe Corridor line, as well as two major new routes radiating northwest and southwest from San Jose, and a long west valley extension to the west of San Jose.

Still another new California light rail system had moved into construction at Los Angeles by late 1985. Work began first on a 21.5-mile line between Los Angeles and Long Beach that is being constructed by the Los Angeles County Transportation Commission (LACTC) almost entirely within the right-of-way that was once utilized by the Pacific Electric Railway's Long Beach interurban line. A downtown Los Angeles subway under Flower Street will carry the line to a junction with Los Angeles' new Metro Rail subway at 7th and Flower streets. A new generation of rail cars should be operating over the line by late 1989. Also under construction is a second LACTC light rail line that should open in 1993 over a 19.5-mile route between Norwalk and Hawthorne in the median of the new Century Freeway. Still other projected light rail routes should eventually extend operation to every major area of Los Angeles County under a rail transit plan that may eventually reach a total of 150 route miles.

At least two other new U.S. light rail systems were close to a construction start. At Dallas, the Dallas Area Rapid Transit was getting ready to begin construction of the first line of a regional light rail system that could eventually reach a total of some 93 miles of line. At St. Louis, final engineering was underway for an 18-mile "Metro Link" light rail line that will link East St. Louis (Ill.), downtown St. Louis, and the suburban areas to the northeast of the city, utilizing the rail deck of the 114-year-old Eads Bridge for its Mississippi River crossing. At least two other St. Louis transportation corridors were likely candidates for additional light rail routes.

In close to 20 other North American cities there were light rail system plans or proposals in varying stages of development. In the east there were light rail schemes being considered for several routes in the New York City area, with plans for a 15-mile New Jersey waterfront system the most advanced. Baltimore was considering two 10-mile light rail routes, extending north and south from the downtown area in existing railroad rights of way. Rochester (N.Y.) had studied an 11-mile light rail project that would utilize the old trolley subway and abandoned railroad right-of-way. At least three different light rail projects had been proposed for Washington (D.C.), including a Dulles Airport connection.

In the south, planning had been started for a 19-mile light rail link between Norfolk and Virginia Beach. Other light rail projects had been proposed for Charlotte, Tampa and New Orleans. In the midwest, preliminary engineering had been completed at Detroit for a 15-mile Woodward Avenue line that could become the initial route for a regional system. At Kansas City consultants had completed early studies for some 23 miles of light rail, while still other studies had been completed at Dayton, Columbus, Milwaukee and the Twin Cities of Minneapolis and St. Paul.

In the southwest, Houston had developed plans for a 75-mile light rail system after voters rejected a planned heavy rapid transit system. At San Antonio early studies had been made for a 31-mile light rail system. Western cities with light rail schemes included Denver, where there were plans for a 17-mile route in railroad rights-of-way, Phoenix, and Seattle.

In Canada, there were tentative plans for a new light rail system at Quebec City, while Mexico was moving ahead with plans for two new light rail systems. Late in 1987 a "turnkey" contract was awarded to Siemens of West Germany for construction of a 10-mile light rail system at Guadalajara, Jalisco, that will replace a trolleybus route located largely in subway. The first 6 miles of line were expected to open late in 1988, with the balance to be completed by early 1989. At Monterrey, Nuevo Leon, a 5-mile light rail route was under consideration.

A whole new generation of electric railway cars had been developed to operate North America's new or rebuilt light rail systems. The earliest such effort, initiated by the Urban Mass Transit Administration in the early 1970's, had been something of a failure.

UMTA's U.S. Standard Light Rail Vehicle (SLRV) was a high capacity, high performance car design that was intended to become a standard for U.S. light rail systems. The SLRV was a 71-foot articulated car of welded low alloy, high tensile steel construction with a seated and standing capacity of well over 200 passengers. Monomotor power trucks were fitted with such features as resilient wheels, and rubber chevron and air spring suspension. Chopper control, two 230 h.p. motors, and a combination of dynamic, disc, and magnetic track brakes contributed to the SLRV's high performance characteristics.

A joint Boston-San Francisco order for 275 of the SLRVs went to Philadelphia aerospace manufacturer Boeing Vertol in 1973. The trouble-plagued SLRV was years late going into service, and never did achieve its original performance and reliability goals. Boston's MBTA ultimately rejected a portion of its 175-car share of the joint order. Although 30 of the rejected Boston cars eventually went to San Francisco, there were no repeat orders for the SLRV.

Another, and more successful, attempt to develop a standardized "new generation" light rail vehicle was initiated by Canada's Urban Transportation Development Corporation (UTDC) during the mid-1970's. UTDC's Canadian Light Rail Vehicle (CLRV) was a 50-foot, double truck car incorporating many of the same kind of advanced features that had been specified for the SLRV. UTDC landed an order for 196 of the single unit version of the CLRV for the Toronto Transit Commission that were delivered during 1979-82. A follow-up order for 52 76-foot articulated versions of the CLRV was delivered to TTC beginning in June 1987, while another 50 86-foot versions of the UTDC articulated were being

supplied during 1987-88 for Santa Clara County's Guadalupe Corridor light rail line.

Philadelphia's Southeastern Pennsylvania Transportation Authority (SEPTA) acquired a fleet of 141 50-foot double truck light rail cars from Japan's Kawasaki Heavy Industries in the early 1980's. The order included 112 single-end cars for SEPTA's West Philadelphia subway-surface lines, while the remainder were double end cars for the former Red Arrow suburban lines operating from 69th Street Terminal in Upper Darby. Buffalo's Niagara Frontier Transportation Authority was the only other system to acquire single unit cars. Japan's Tokyu Car Corporation supplied a fleet of 27 unusually large, 67-foot double end cars in 1984 for NFTA's Metro Rail light rail rapid transit system.

For a majority of the new or rebuilt light rail systems, however, the double-end, articulated car seemed to be the clear preference for new vehicle orders. Thus far, the closest thing to a standard articulated light rail vehicle has proved to be the German-built Siemens/Duewag U2 car originally developed for Frankfurt, Germany. The U2 was a 76-foot, double-end car incorporating advanced design and performance features. From the late 1970's through early 1988, nearly 200 U2 cars had been delivered, or were on order, for the new light rail systems at Edmonton, Calgary, San Diego, and Sacramento, while Pittsburgh's rebuilt PAT light rail system acquired 55 of the slightly larger Siemens/Duewag U3 articulated car. In Mexico, a fleet of 16 Siemens/Duewag articulated cars for Guadalajara's new light rail line was being assembled by Constructora Nacional de Carros de Ferrocarril (CNCF) at Mexico City.

There were still other articulated light rail vehicle suppliers, too. Italy's Breda Costruzioni Ferroviarie built 48 articulated cars for Cleveland's rebuilt Shaker Heights light rail system in 1982, while Canada's Bombardier supplied 26 articulated units for Portland's Banfield line that were constructed under a license from Belgium's BN. After its unhappy experience with the Boeing Vertol SLRV, Boston's MBTA developed a "second generation" articulated light rail car that combined many of the SLRV's best features with a variety of improvements intended to greatly enhance performance and reliability. A hundred of these Type 7 Surface

Railcars were supplied to MBTA's Green Line system by Japan's Kinki Sharyo during 1986-87. Still another overseas supplier successfully entered the North American light rail vehicle marketplace in 1987 when Japan's Sumitomo/Nippon Sharyo landed an order to supply a fleet of 87-foot, articulated cars for Los Angeles County. The order provided for delivery of 54 cars during 1989-90, with an option for an additional 42 cars.

Several of the rebuilt light rail systems continued to rely upon the durable PCC car for at least part of their equipment needs. Both Boston and Philadelphia had augmented their new car fleets with extensively rebuilt PCC car fleets. Toronto rebuilt a substantial portion of its retained PCC car fleet during the 1970's, and was considering the feasibility of a second rebuild program for a PCC car fleet that would operate the new Harbourfront light rail line. In the early 1980's Pittsburgh began what amounted to a complete remanufacturing program for a 45-car PCC fleet that would augment its new LRV's. The rebuilt cars were expected to continue in service through the end of the century.

Newark's City Subway light rail line continued to rely exclusively on its 40-year-old PCC car fleet. Meticulous maintenance and a heavy overhaul program were expected to keep the cars in reliable service well into the 1990's. Mexico City, too, stayed out of the new equipment market. Instead, the city's Service de Transportes Electricos del D.F. had begun to rebuild its PCC car fleet into modern eight-axle, three-section articulated cars for operation on STE's rebuilt and expanded light rail system.

In addition to an unprecedented level of interest in new light rail systems, there was lively activity in tourist-oriented historic trolley projects in a number of North American cities. The historic trolley boom had started in Detroit, where a mile-and-a-quarter line had opened in 1976 as part of the city's downtown revival efforts. Former Lisbon, Portugal, cars and a British double-deck car operated on the narrow gauge line. At Lowell, Massachusetts, three replica cars operated on a mile-long route, while former Red Arrow cars were operating on a mile of track on the Philadelphia waterfront. Former Brussels streetcars were being operated on a 3.5-mile resort line at Orlando, Florida. A single car operated over a two-mile line at French Lick, Indiana. A former San Antonio trolley ran over several blocks of electric freight track operated by the city's Pearl Brewery, while a Fort Collins, Colorado, Birney had been restored to tourist service on part of one of the city's original trolley routes. Two former Portuguese trolleys were being operated at Yakima, Washington, while four ex-Australian trams were in service on 1.5 miles of Seattle waterfront track. Similar operations were under construction or planned at Richmond, Galveston, Dallas, Phoenix, and Tucson.

At San Francisco a Market Street "Historic Trolley Festival" originally operated in 1983 as a substitute for temporarily inactive cable cars had become a permanent fixture, and the city was considering a rehabilitated fleet of PCC cars to operate a similar service on its planned new Embarcadero line. Toronto operated old Peter Witt cars in a tourist-oriented summer "Tour Tram" service. Similar historic car operations were being readied for downtown operation by the new light rail systems at Portland and San Jose.

Surely it was all a promising beginning for the second century of the electric street railway.

Leading into 1938, the street railway industry was in trouble. Perhaps the most visible signs were cars long past their economic useful life and in many cases totally lacking in esthetics. ABOVE: Hot Springs (Arkansas) Street Railway car 30 shows its lineage from early horse cars in its design. However, there is evidence of marketing. Nonstop service to the track requires a premium of three cents over the regular seven cent fare. ADJACENT PAGE TOP LEFT: The blunt design of a Barber Car product is evident in the presence of Black River Traction Co. car 1. This photograph was taken at State Street and Park Terrace at Watertown, New York, on June 23, 1936. TOP RIGHT: Fonda Johnstown & Groversville car 25 was still in service in 1936. Note the track brake. BOTTOM: On the last day of service, car 222 of Spokane (Washington) United Railways was wearily grinding out the miles. *(All photos Krambles Collection)*

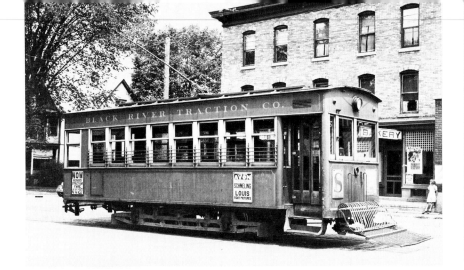

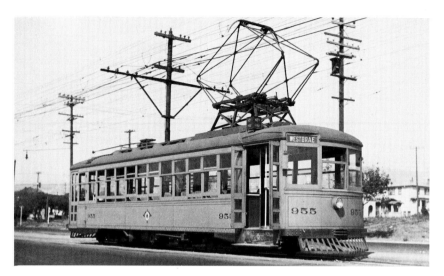 

ADJACENT PAGE TOP LEFT: Car 955 was built by American Car Co. of St. Louis in 1926 for $11,460. It was equipped with a pantograph, steel pilot and whistles for operation on the Westbrae shuttle of the Key System. The shuttle service was terminated in 1941, after which this car returned to streetcar service in the Oakland, California, area. TOP LEFT: Yakima (Washington) Valley Transportation Co. 20 was one of three Master Units built by J. G. Brill Company in 1930. This was one of the modest modern streetcar designs. BOTTOM: Birmingham (Alabama) Electric Co. car 50 can best be described as ugly. However, this represents still another design—in this case, a "Jim Crow car," with segregated seating for white people in front and "colored people" in the back. *(All photos Krambles Collection)* THIS PAGE TOP: Peter Witt was the street railway commissioner in Cleveland. He designed this type of car, which first appeared in Cleveland in 1914. The car was designed for lines with heavy traffic that rode short distances. Car 929 is in service on the Wellston line of St. Louis Public Service. *(RVM photo)* Louisville Railway's 1085, at 4th and Broadway in that Kentucky city in September, 1938, represents the streetcar design that was introduced circa 1910. *(Glenn W. Nicely photo Krambles Collection)*

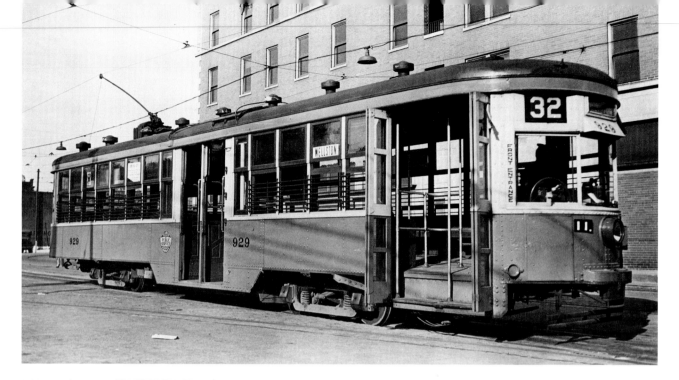

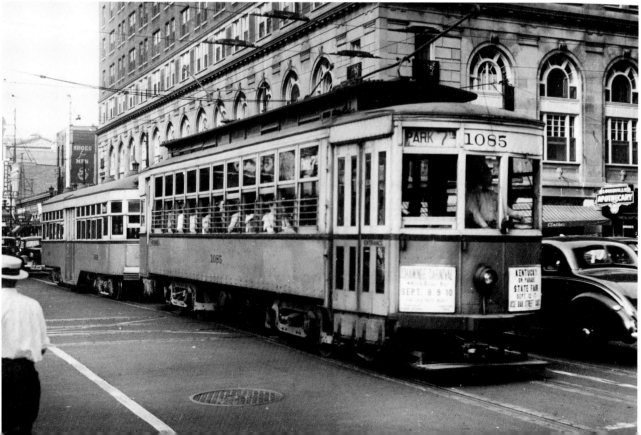

LEFT: Cumberland County Power & Light Co. car 254 is a class Brill designed and built car. The slight arch in the window is reminiscent of car designs of the 1890's. However, many operators had cars of this design era to the end of service. On January 6, 1940, this car was in service in Portland, Maine. BELOW: Stone & Webster had many streetcar properties in small cities which needed a lightweight car. The result was the "Birney," shown here on the Sacramento & Northern in Chico, California. These cars were the rage of the 1920's, an era in which operators wanted to save money. (*Both photos Krambles Collection*)

The first true standard streetcar was the President's Conference Committee car, or PCC. The first PCC car entered revenue service in Pittsburgh in 1936. Car 3018 was built for the Boston Elevated Railway Company by Pullman Standard Car Mfg. Co. of Worchester, Massachusetts, in March, 1941. What distinguished the PCC were the trucks and car body, which were the result of research by a committee representing streetcar companies in the United States and Canada. (All Pullman Standard photos from GK Collection)

23

LEFT: The early 1940's were years of stability for the remaining streetcar lines. Car 55 was in service for the Roanoke (Virginia) Railway & Electric Company, circa 1940. ADJACENT PAGE TOP: Car 803 was in service in Richmond, Virginia, in 1942. However, this car was built for service in South Bend, Indiana. BOTTOM: Pacific Electric 692 was one of 160 "Hollywood" cars for suburban service in the Los Angeles area. On April 7, 1944, this car was in service on the Hollywood Avenue line. *(All three photos WCJ)* BELOW: On Sunday, August 24, 1941, Indiana Service Corporation car 542 is passing the Allen County Courthouse in Ft. Wayne, Indiana. It seems so tranquil in all of these views. *(John F. Humiston photo)*

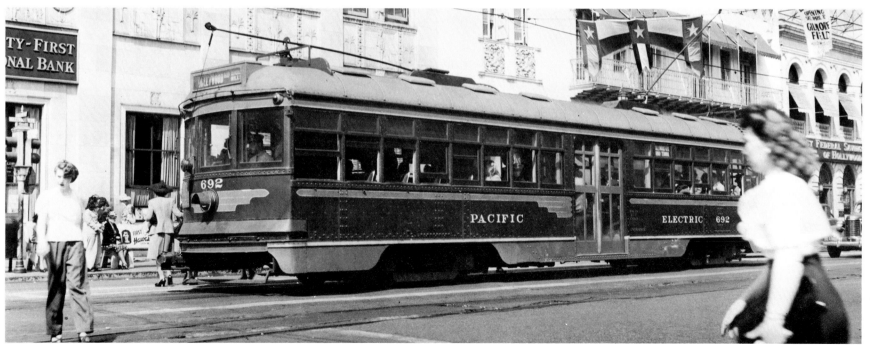

The years following World War II were a period of transition for street railways. Not only was the rolling stock reaching the end of its useful life, but the power distribution systems and the rest of the infrastructure of the systems were in need of renewal. Much has been made of the "conspiracy" of General Motors, tire companies and gasoline companies to replace streetcars with buses. The reality of economic life was that these suppliers offered a financing solution to street railway operators which streetcar manufacturers and power distribution equipment suppliers did not. ADJACENT PAGE TOP: In September, 1946,

Pittsburgh Railways 1154 is at 10th and Liberty Ave. on a Route 44, Knoxville, run. BOTTOM: Both Montreal and Vancouver offered sightseeing car rides. Montreal Tramways Car 2 is on Queen Mary Road passing the St. Joseph's Oratory on June 17, 1947. ABOVE: Some of the lines of the Philadelphia Suburban Transportation Co. (Red Arrow Lines) survive in the 1980's. But car 21 and friend and the West Chester line are a part of history. This scene on West Chester Place at Eagle Road dates to August 30, 1949. Streetcar service to West Chester ended on June 4, 1954, when buses took over. *(All WCJ)*

FACING PAGE: Anaconda Cooper Mining Co. Opportunity line train is outbound at the junction with the Smelter line on the east side of Anaconda, near 3rd and Jefferson streets. Above the car is the Butte, Anaconda & Pacific Railway. These cars date from 1901. Service ended in December, 1951, eighteen months after this photo was taken by *Charles Smallwood* in July, 1949. *(GK*

Collection) ABOVE: While best known for its part in designing the Birney car, Stone & Webster also designed this car type, which earned the nickname of "turtle-back" because of its distinctive roof design. Dallas Railway & Terminal Company cars 437 and 439 meet on State at Clark when *Thomas H. Desnoyers* was there on August 14, 1948. *(Krambles Collection)*

Following World War II, a combination of need and optimism caused some street railway operators to order PCC cars. The postwar PCC cars were all-electric cars and easily distinguished by the standee windows in the roof line. Birmingham (Alabama) Electric Co. ordered 48 PCC cars from Pullman Standard to reequip the six trolley lines that would be retained. In April, 1953, streetcar operations had ended in Birmingham and the PCC cars went to Toronto. *(All photos Pullman Standard from Carlson Collection and underside view from Krambles Collection)* NEXT PAGE TOP: In the 1950's, it was becoming obvious which properties would survive. The Toronto Transportation Commission would retain streetcar service, though the venerable Peter Witts, like 2936, would be retired. Car 2936 and trailer are serving on the Yonge line at Front and Bay streets on June 15, 1950. BOTTOM RIGHT: Twin Cities Rapid Transit was noted for its distinctive home-built cars. Cars 1216 and 1241 are on the Hazle Park—North St. Paul route on September 22, 1951. *(Both photos WCJ)* BOTTOM LEFT: Chicago had the largest street railway system but the last car operated early on June 22, 1958. In July, 1951, car 5095 is on the Racine line at 64th Street. *(RVM)*

FACING PAGE TOP: Throughout the 20th Century, Market Street in San Francisco has been identified with streetcars. In 1988, regular service cars are in a tunnel below while the Historic Trolley service operates at surface level. Some people wish there would be regular service on the surface level. On June 1, 1951, Municipal Railways car 1014 is heading south on Market Street. Car 1014 is one of ten double-end cars delivered by St. Louis Car Co. in 1948. They were wired for multiple unit operation but never received couplers. Initially, these were assigned to the Judah Line. (WCJ) BOTTOM: Los Angeles' transportation policy has been influenced by the automobile for years. The street railway system came to an end in 1963. Perhaps the major reason was that people would simply rather drive than ride. During the 1950's, the number of streetcars required for service declined by over 50%. This was not a result of line abandonment but rather was due to a loss of riders. In December, 1953, car 1438 is southbound on Main Street at First, passing Los Angeles' landmark Civic Center. (WDM)

The 1960's were the dark days of trolley operations in the United States. Cities with streetcar operations at the end of the sixties were Boston, Newark, Pittsburgh, Philadelphia, New Orleans, Fort Worth, El Paso, San Francisco and Shaker Heights (Cleveland), Ohio. In Newark, 24 PCC cars serve on a five-mile line from Penn Station to Franklin Street. The line was rehabilitated in the early 1980s. The operation in Fort Worth was essentially a shuttle between a parking lot and a downtown department store. The El Paso operation came to an end in May, 1974, after 15 years of sporadic operation in neighboring Juarez. While streetcars remained in Philadelphia, things have been anything but bright. Southeastern Pennsylvania Transportation Authority (SEPTA), successor to Philadelphia Transportation Co., has chronically suffered from a shortage of funds. This has resulted in terminating service due to deteriorated rolling stock and track structures. On April 12, 1964, car 2650 is on the loop at 63rd Street and Malvern, the west end of the number 10 line. The number 10 line is one of the West Philadelphia subway-surface routes that is still operated in 1988 by SEPTA. *(WDM)*

ABOVE LEFT: A tale of two rush hours. In the West, people line up on Market Street to board a trolley that served one of five lines that in 1988 still travel on Market Street, albeit in a subway now. On August 6, 1979, car 1010 is serving on the "J" Church line on Market Street at Powell during the afternoon rush period. San Francisco's famous Emporium department store provides the background. Late in 1987, San Francisco received a Federal grant to fund an $18 million, 2.3-mile extension of the "J" line from its terminal at 30th Street and Church via 30th Street and San Jose Avenue to the Metro Center. The first revenue service over the extension is expected in late 1990. ABOVE RIGHT: A line of PCC cars on Queen Street opposite the new City Hall in Toronto on June 2, 1980. Toronto had more PCC cars than any other property. Between 1938 and 1957, Toronto Transportation Commission acquired 745 PCC cars, both new and used. Acquisition of 205 used cars occurred from 1950 to 1957. The cars came from Cincinnati (52), Cleveland (75), Birmingham (48) and Kansas City (30). Replacement of the PCC cars commenced in the form of the Canadian Light Rail Vehicle (CLRV), which entered service in 1979. (WDM)

During the 1970's, streetcars in the United States were truly in the doldrums—but not in Pittsburgh. In a travel through history, we will review the transition from old to new and from traditional paint schemes to perhaps a riot of colors and the strangest streetcar livery of all. ADJACENT PAGE TOP LEFT: In virtually a timeless scene, PAT 1613 approached Library on March 26, 1977. This is near the point to where the "interurban line" to Charleroi, Pennsylvania, was cut back on June 29, 1953. The car is still in the traditional red and cream paint scheme of Pittsburgh Railways. BOTTOM LEFT: The standard scheme, if there was one, was this vertical combination of colors, which could range from purple through orange, yellow, green and blue to basic white. Car 1785 is rounding the corner of Arlington and Warrington in the community of Mt. Washington on July 10, 1977. TOP RIGHT: The Bi-Centennial was recognized by painting car 1791, which is seen entering Broadway Avenue in Beechview, Pennsylvania, on February 17, 1979. BOTTOM RIGHT: When PAT could no longer obtain body parts, the shop crews resorted to fabricating a front end from standard steel shapes. This "extra special trolley" became one of a few traveling billboards. Car 1779 is passing the Pittsburgh & Lake Erie Railway station on July 9, 1977. ABOVE: The height, or the depth, of the trolley design scheme was car 1794, the "Triple Treat" car, complete with a sheet metal "upper deck" and "smoke stacks." This car was actually part of a sightseeing trip that included the three attractions shown on the side of the car. With all of its additions, the car would not fit into the South Mills Tunnel, so it could get in and out of downtown only on the Warrington Avenue trackage. On August 13, 1977, car 1794 is at the South Mills car house. *(All photos Gordon E. Lloyd)*

37

We will start a tour of those operations which provide service in 1988. LEFT: Boston's Green Line is prospering. The system includes the downtown subway which leads to four branch lines plus the Ashment-Mattapan extension of the Red Line. The system includes 35 miles of route and over 200 vehicles. Beginning in 1986, MBTA started to receive the first of 100 of these light rail vehicles, which are built by Kinki Sharyo. Together with the Boeing Standard Light Rail Vehicles (SLRV), these cars provide the daily service. On October 26, 1986, car 3617 was at Newton Highlands, Maine. *(Norton D. Clark photo)* BELOW: Toronto is a Mecca for light rail. In 1988, service is provided by 196 of these Canadian Light Rail Vehicles (CLRV) plus approximately 60 PCC cars that remain from Toronto's fleet of 745 cars, and 52 Articulated Canadian Light Rail Vehicles (ALRV). The first CLRV arrived on December 29, 1977. This was one of six prototypes manufactured by Swiss Industrial Company (SIG). The production order of 190 cars was awarded to Hawker Siddeley, which delivered the cars between April 24, 1979, and November 19, 1981. Revenue service for the CLRV's commenced on September 30, 1979, on Route 507, "Long Branch." Car 4037 is providing this service at the Long Branch terminal on May 31, 1980. The next order of cars will be completed in 1989. On January 19, 1988, the first of 52 ALRVs entered service on Route 507 *(WDM)*.

ABOVE LEFT: Philadelphia's streetcar system is divided into two segments—surface routes, which are operated with PCC cars, and the routes from West Philadelphia which share the Market Street subway. The prototype of the Kawasaki cars that serve these subway-surface routes arrived in Philadelphia on July 29, 1980, and entered revenue service on October 10, 1980. The balance of the 112-car order was delivered between 1981 and 1983. While the future of the subway-surface lines seems secure, the surface routes have generally been contracted over the years. They may yet be victims of deferred maintenance. Car 9058 is approaching the Woodland Avenue entrance to the subway on December

9, 1985. ABOVE RIGHT: Light rail service returned to Buffalo when the new rail rapid transit line opened on May 20, 1985. The downtown section of the line has been in limited service since October, 1984. Tokyo Car Corp. manufactured 27 double-end cars for this service. The line is 6.4 miles long. With the exception of 1.3 miles in downtown, the line is in a subway. Ridership is growing and the agency is interested in additional rolling stock. Car 102 is northbound on the Main Street Mall at Lafayette Square. The mall was still under construction when this photo was taken on November 5, 1984, shortly after the service began on the mall. (Two photos WDM)

LEFT: In 1982, 48 articulated railcars built by Breda Costruzione Ferroviarie SpA entered service on Cleveland's Blue Line and Green Line light rail routes. These lines are more commonly referred to as the Shaker Heights Rapid Transit lines. On January 11, 1986, car 844 is operating inbound to Public Square at 34th Street. From 55th Street to downtown, the Shaker cars share the rails with Cleveland's Red Line "heavy rail" rapid transit trains. BELOW: In Pittsburgh, PCC cars still operate on the Library line, but service on the route via Mt. Lebanon is provided by a fleet of 55 LRV's built by Siemens/Duewag Car 4118 is in the streets of Mt. Lebanon on April 3, 1987, prior to entering revenue service on May 22, 1987. The new service includes new trackage across the former Pennsylvania Railroad's Panhandle bridge into a short subway into the Gateway Center complex. *(Two photos WDM)* FACING PAGE TOP LEFT: Light rail operations were introduced to Western Canada on April 23, 1978, when operations commenced between downtown and the northeast section of Edmonton. In 1981, there was a modest extension further to the northeast which resulted

in a 6.4-mile system that is operated with 37 Siemens/Duewag cars. Plans have been drawn for extensions to the south. In October, 1986, car 1034 is entering the subway on its trip downtown. LEFT: In 1988 Calgary operates three light rail lines which are named for the direction they travel from the central business district; South, Northeast and Northwest. Operations in Calgary began on May 25, 1981, when the 7.7-mile South Line was opened from Anderson Road north to downtown. On April 27, 1985, a second line, 6.1 miles long to Whitehorn in the Northeast section, was opened. On September 4, 1987, the Northwest Line to the stadium was opened in time to serve the 1988 Winter Olympics. In December, 1986, car 2048, one of 83 Siemens/Duewag cars, is departing the Bridgeland Memorial station on the Northeast line. Extensions of all three existing lines, plus additional lines, are contemplated. ABOVE: Light rail service began in Portland in September, 1986, over a route which, in part, was a former interurban line of the Portland Traction Company. Ridership on this line to Gresham has exceeded projections. Shortly after the line opened, car 102, one of 26 cars built by Bombardier under a license from BN of Belgium, is at Southwest 1st Street and Southwest Yamhill in downtown Portland. Studies of extensions are under way. *(Three photos John Harder)*

41

It is hard to believe that in California, the kingdom of the automobile, there are now four light rail systems—San Diego, San Francisco, Sacramento and San Jose. More incredible is that someone has suggested connecting the San Francisco and San Jose lines. As *Passenger Train Journal* noted, "We think this concept is called an interurban." While San Francisco has had street railway operation continuously since 1891, the modern era began on July 26, 1981, when the San Diego Trolley, a subsidiary of the Metropolitan Transit Development Board (MTDB), began revenue service. BELOW: Car 1006 is at the San Ysidro Terminal, which is located on the U. S.-Mexican border, on July 15, 1982. Fifteen miles ahead is the San Diego terminal, which is adjacent to the Amtrak (Santa Fe) station. In 1988, construction is under way on the Euclid line extension to El Cajon. The Bayside line and other extensions are planned. (*WDM*)

TOP LEFT: Light rail operations began in Sacramento in March, 1987, when RTD Metro began operations on the Watt/I-80 (northern leg) of its "U"-shaped system. Service to Butterfield on the Folsom Corridor began on September 5, 1987. Car 120 is inbound on the Folsom Corridor near 47th Street on January 25, 1988. BOTTOM LEFT: Late in 1988, construction is scheduled to begin on an extension of the "J" Church line of San Francisco's Municipal Railways (Muni). Construction will extend the line from 30th Street and Church, where this Boeing SLRV is turning on January 27, 1988, to the Metro Center facility at Geneva and San Jose. RIGHT: Light rail operations by Santa Clara County Transit District commenced on December, 1987, when service began from the maintenance facility to Tasman-Old Ironsides in Santa Clara. On June 16, 1988, service was extended through downtown San Jose to the Convention Center. From this point, construction will begin on a line to the Santa Teresa station down the Almaden Corridor. UTDC-built car 815 is leaving the Lick Mill station. Tasman Drive had yet to be completed when this photo was taken on January 22, 1988. *(All photos WDM)*

43

CHAPTER 2

THE INTERURBAN VANISHES...ALMOST

If the street railway industry had come on hard times by the end of the 1930's, the electric interurbans were in far worse difficulties. Indeed, by any reasonable standard, the interurbans were clearly a dying industry.

Developed from the same direct current technology as the street railways, the interurbans had enjoyed only a brief period of growth and profitability early in the century. Construction of new lines had virtually ceased by the beginning of World War I, when the interurbans reached a peak of about 18,000 miles, and the industry soon began a period of continuing decline. After World War I there was an increasing rate of abandonment as the more marginal lines began to fail. Orders for new equipment fell steadily. Both gross operating revenues and net earnings began a long-term decline.

The cause of the interurbans' failure, of course, was the private automobile. The interurbans had been developed largely for short-haul passenger traffic, a market that proved even more susceptible to the automobile than urban transit passengers. As automobile sales reached record levels after the war, and the good roads movement of the 1920's paralleled the interurbans with a network of paved highways, the passenger traffic upon which the electric lines depended began to vanish.

By the beginning of the Great Depression, fully 25 percent of the American interurban network had already been abandoned. A once-extensive network of roadside rural trolley lines in New England was largely gone. In New York and Michigan, both of which had enjoyed widespread interurban systems, most of the intercity electric lines had been abandoned, or would be within another few years. In Ohio and Indiana, which had the greatest of all interurban systems, comprehensive, statewide networks were beginning to disintegrate.

Just as they had for the street railway industry, the adversities of the 1920's had encouraged efforts to modernize the interurban industry with improved equipment and services, and to reduce operating costs. Although these efforts produced nothing for the interurbans that came even close to matching the beneficial impact of the PCC car on the street railways, there had been some notable successes. At Chicago, for example, utilities entrepreneur Samuel Insull had applied extensive rehabilitation, new equipment, and innovative services to the three principal interurbans radiating from the city—the Chicago North Shore & Milwaukee, the Chicago South Shore & South Bend, and the Chicago, Aurora & Elgin—to remake them into model heavy duty electric railways.

The advances in lightweight car design that had developed during the 1920's, together with the development of much lighter weight traction motors, had been combined at the beginning of the 1930's to produce some radically improved high-speed, lightweight interurban cars. In Ohio and Indiana two encouraging attempts to establish state-wide interurban systems from some of the stronger properties—the Cincinnati & Lake Erie Railroad and the Indiana Railroad—had employed large fleets of new lightweight, high-speed cars as a principal element of their efforts to revive the failing interurban systems in the two states. At Philadelphia, new lightweight, high-speed Brill "Bullet" cars had been acquired to help restore the Philadelphia & Western to a competitive position; an additional fleet of smaller "Bullets" went to the Fonda, Johnstown & Gloversville, one of the few New York interurbans to survive much beyond the beginning of the depression.

Despite such efforts, things rapidly grew worse for the interurbans as the depression advanced. For a sample of 40 interurban lines, 1930 net operating revenues were down by 46 percent from the previous year. For 1931 another sample of 29 companies showed operating revenues down an average of 22 percent from those for 1930, and some lines reported decreases of as much as 60 percent. A survey of financial reports for 1931 showed that only six of 23 companies had any net income at all.

Given operating results like these, the decline of the industry only accelerated. During the first five years of the depression over 5000 miles of interurban line were abandoned; at the beginning of

1935 less than half of the 1917 peak of just over 18,000 miles of interurban lines was left. Even the strongest of the Insull interurbans at Chicago were not immune to the reverses of the failing national economy. After its gross operating revenues fell to less than half the 1929 level in only three years, the North Shore Line went into bankruptcy in 1932. The South Shore Line, which had experienced a comparable reduction in gross operating revenues, followed the North Shore into receivership a year later.

By the end of the decade, less than a third of the original U.S. interurban network remained. The two brave attempts to salvage something of the great traction systems of Ohio and Indiana had failed. The C&LE shut down what was left of its Ohio River to the Great Lakes system early in 1939, while the Indiana Railroad abandoned the last parts of its statewide system in 1940 and 1941. The Fonda, Johnstown & Gloversville's attempt to revive its interurban passenger traffic with fast new cars also failed, and the line abandoned its interurban operations in 1938 after its Mohawk River bridge at Schenectady was condemned.

With but few exceptions, the prototypical interurban railways that had depended primarily upon short-haul, intercity passenger traffic for their revenues were gone by the end of the 1930's. Most of the lines that continued to operate owed their survival to special circumstances of one kind or another.

For most of them, the development of a substantial carload freight business, interchanged with the steam railroads, had provided the extra margin of earnings that made continued electric passenger operation possible. In Iowa, for example, the interurbans had been developed largely as short line feeders to the steam railroads, with an appreciable carload freight traffic from the very beginning, and the state's interurban system remained almost intact. In the Southeast, the important Piedmont & Northern lines in North and South Carolina continued to operate for similar reasons. In the West, particularly, many of the interurbans had been developed with freight, as much as passengers, in mind. The four Utah interurbans centered on Ogden and Salt Lake City, and California's Sacramento Northern, were important examples.

A particularly notable system that survived largely because of freight traffic was the Illinois Terminal Railroad, which extended north and east from St. Louis to Springfield, Peoria, Decatur, Champaign-Urbana, and Danville. Originally operated as a typical passenger-oriented interurban, the IT had set out very early to develop freight bypass routes and other improvements that permitted the company to become a major carload freight carrier.

At a number of major urban areas in the U.S. and Canada, interurbans survived through the end of the 1930's largely as suburban passenger carriers. At Philadelphia, the Philadelphia Suburban Transportation Company and the Philadelphia & Western Railroad operated several routes that linked the city's western suburbs with the 69th Street elevated terminal. The Pittsburgh Railways operated suburban service south of the city over two interurban routes that were extensions of the company's extensive streetcar system. At Atlanta, the Georgia Railway & Power Company operated two similar interurban routes to Stone Mountain and Marietta. The Milwaukee Electric lines continued to operate three major interurban routes that linked the city with its suburbs and nearby cities to the south, west, and north. In Canada, the Montreal & Southern Counties, a Canadian National subsidiary, had become an important suburban carrier between the city and the suburbs south of the St. Lawrence.

Several of these remaining urban area interurbans had also developed a substantial base of freight traffic, in addition to their suburban passenger business. The three major Chicago interurbans once controlled by Samuel Insull, for example, had all established a very substantial interchange freight traffic with their steam railroad connections. The Pacific Electric Railway at Los Angeles, which operated the largest interurban passenger service in North America, had also developed the heaviest freight traffic of any interurban, serving as a feeder to its parent Southern Pacific Company.

Elsewhere in North America, there was a scattering of hardy survivors of the interurban era. In New England, very little was left. In northern Maine the Aroostook Valley Railroad, a Canadian Pacific subsidiary, continued to haul lumber, potatoes, and a few passengers. At Springfield, Vermont, the little Springfield Terminal Railway provided the city with a freight and passenger link to the Boston & Maine at nearby Charleston, N.H.

Abandonment of the Fonda, Johnston & Gloversville in 1938

had left New York with only the Jamestown, Westfield & Northwestern, an interurban in the western part of the state that had originally been a steam railroad. New Jersey, too, had only a single remaining interurban, the Atlantic City & Shore, which linked the resort centers of Atlantic City and Ocean City. Pennsylvania had considerably more surviving interurban properties. With the exception of the Lackawanna & Wyoming Valley, a third rail line that handled both carload freight and passenger traffic between Scranton and Wilkes Barre, the remaining Pennsylvania lines had somehow managed to continue operating without the carload freight that sustained most of the surviving North American interurbans. Centered on Allentown, the Lehigh Valley Transit Company operated interurban routes to Easton and Philadelphia. In the Pennsylvania Dutch country Hershey Transit and the Conestoga Transportation Company continued to operate a number of rural trolley lines, while the West Penn Railways operated an extensive system of intercity trolley routes in the coke region of western Pennsylvania.

In Maryland, the Hagerstown & Frederick operated several rural trolley lines, while the Baltimore & Annapolis, a surviving section of the great Washington, Baltimore & Annapolis system, provided the only available rail freight and passenger service between the two cities. West Virginia's Monongahela-West Penn operated between Clarksburg and Weston, while the Tri-City Traction Company linked Princeton and Bluefield with a short interurban line.

Texas and Oklahoma retained several important interurbans. The Dallas-centered Texas Electric Railway operated freight and passenger service north to Denison and south to Waco. The Oklahoma Railway's interurban lines linked the state's capitol city with El Reno, Guthrie and Norman. The Sand Springs Railway operated from Tulsa to nearby Sand Springs, while the Pittsburg County Railroad handled a heavy coal traffic and a few passengers in southeast Oklahoma. Still another surviving Oklahoma line, the Union Traction Company, operated north from Nowata to Independence and Parsons, Kansas.

Aside from the four Utah lines, only a single interurban remained in the Mountain States. This was the novel Denver & Intermountain, which operated both standard and narrow gauge routes from Denver to nearby Golden. On the West Coast, the Portland Electric Power Company continued to operate interurban routes east and south from the city, including a route to Oregon City that was generally regarded as the first true interurban.

In Canada there were a number of interurban survivors, almost all of them because of a significant freight traffic. At Vancouver, the British Columbia Electric Railway operated an extensive suburban service, as well as a long interurban route to Chilliwack. In Ontario, several lines linked ports on the north shore of Lake Erie with the cities and the east-west steam railroads to the north. The London & Port Stanley linked the latter port with St. Thomas and London. Two Canadian Pacific-controlled lines, the Lake Erie & Northern and the Grand River Railway, operated north from Port Dover to Brantford, Preston and Kitchener. The Canadian National's Niagara, St. Catharines & Toronto operated across the peninsula just west of Buffalo and Niagara Falls, linking St. Catharines with Port Dalhousie on Lake Ontario and Port Colborne on Lake Erie. At Quebec City a surviving interurban route of the Quebec Railway, Light & Power Company transported pilgrimage traffic to the great Roman Catholic shrine at Ste. Anne de Beaupre, and provided the only link between the transcontinental Canadian National system and its isolated Murray Bay subdivision.

Along the north central coast of Cuba a notable example of the typical heavy electric interurban railway continued to operate between Havana and Matanzas. This was the Hershey Cuban Railway, built by the Hershey Chocolate Corporation after World War I both as a transportation link for its vast Cuban sugar enterprise and as a freight and passenger common carrier.

With more than two-thirds of the industry already gone by the end of the depression decade, and most of the survivors in a precarious state of economic health, it was hard to be very optimistic about the future of the interurban at the end of the 1930's. But occasionally there were a few encouraging developments.

Abandonment of some of the properties that had modernized at the beginning of the decade had made available some excellent rolling stock that made its way to several of the surviving lines. The five lightweight, high-speed Brill "Bullet" cars built for the Fonda, Johnstown & Gloversville, for example, went into high speed service between Ogden and Salt Lake City on Utah's Bamberger Railroad. After the Cincinnati & Lake Erie ended operations in 1939, its fleet of lightweight, high-speed cars was divided between Iowa's Cedar Rapids & Iowa City and Pennsylvania's Lehigh Valley Transit. The same two roads each obtained one of the Indiana Railroad's similar cars; the remainder of IRR's 35-car fleet, unfortunately, was broken up for its aluminum scrap content on the eve of World War II.

Many of the lightweight cars built for a number of roads during the 1920's also moved on to new owners. Lightweight cars from two abandoned Indiana and Illinois lines helped to upgrade service on the Oklahoma Railway, while similar equipment from New York and Indiana went to Oregon's Portland Electric Power Company interurban routes. The curved side lightweight cars built in large numbers by the Cincinnati Car Company proved particularly popular on the used equipment market. Some sort of record was set by several of these cars built for the Indianapolis & Southeastern in 1928; by the time they were scrapped in 1951, five of them had operated on no less than four different properties.

If they were neither particularly new nor modern, heavy steel cars from several abandoned properties went on to new owners. The Chicago, Aurora & Elgin, for example, was able to augment its mixed wood and steel car fleet in 1938 with eight steel cars from the Washington, Baltimore & Annapolis. In 1939 the Des Moines & Central Iowa Railroad replaced its aging wooden passenger cars with three steel cars from Ohio's Lake Shore Electric.

After a dearth of new car orders through most of the Great Depression, a few roads even bought new cars. In 1940 Pacific Electric bought 30 double-end, multiple unit PCC cars for its Glendale-Burbank route and the Venice Short Line. A year later, the Philadelphia Suburban Transportation Company bought ten new lightweight cars that were to prove the last cars ever built by the great Philadelphia car builder, J.G. Brill.

The most notable new equipment acquisition, however, was by the Chicago North Shore & Milwaukee. Bankrupt since 1932, the North Shore came out of a 51-day strike in 1938 dangerously close to abandonment. Instead, the line's receiver elected to initiate a massive program for passenger traffic recovery. Two splendid articulated *Electroliner* trains delivered by St. Louis Car early in 1941 were the centerpiece of the rehabilitated North Shore passenger service. Streamlined and air conditioned, the 85 m.p.h. *Electroliners* were, quite simply, the finest electric interurban passenger equipment ever built. Modernized standard equipment complemented the *Electroliners* in the company's refurbished Chicago-Milwaukee service.

On the North Shore, too, there was even some new construction. A project completed late in 1940 provided the line's Shore Line Route trains with a new four-mile, grade-separated route through the North Shore suburbs of Glencoe, Winnetka, and Kenilworth.

World War II brought a temporary halt to the decline of America's surviving interurbans, for the same reasons that it had for the street railways. Freight and passenger travel were both up with the booming wartime economy, and wartime shortages severely curtailed automobile travel. On the South Shore Line, for example, passenger travel had doubled the 1941 level by 1943. And by 1945 the South Shore was carrying more than six million passengers, almost double the level of 1929, the best year ever in the company's pre-war history. The North Shore Line's passenger traffic climbed from just over ten million revenue passengers in 1940 to a wartime peak of almost 28 million in 1945. The enormous growth in Southern California's defense industries sent Pacific Electric Railway passenger traffic to record levels. From less than 43 million passengers in 1940, PE rail traffic grew to over 100 million by 1945, the highest level in the company's history.

Representative of the smaller lines particularly hard pressed by wartime traffic demands was the Oklahoma Railway, which handled a heavy volume of passengers generated by both defense industries and a huge U.S. Navy training base at Norman. Service on the Norman line was doubled to more than 40 daily runs, with some trips operated with four or more sections.

The interurbans sought rolling stock for this surge of traffic anywhere they could. The Chicago, Aurora & Elgin leased old wooden cars from the North Shore Line, while the North Shore itself rebuilt idle parlor and dining cars into coaches. In 1942 the South Shore Line began a program of lengthening its 60 and 61 foot steel cars by 17 feet 6 inches, adding anywhere from 24 to 30 seats per car. By 1946, 23 cars had been rebuilt in this manner. The Pacific Electric overhauled nearly a hundred of its old wooden cars for wartime traffic. Some of these—in PE's 950-999 class—were literally pulled off the scrap line; 19 cars were already gone when the decision to rebuild the class for wartime service was made. In 1942, PE was able to expand its interurban passenger roster with 80 big steel or aluminum suburban cars acquired from abandoned Southern Pacific and Northwestern Pacific lines in the San Francisco Bay area. The Oklahoma Railway was so desperate for rolling stock that it converted four freight cars to passenger service in 1943, while another eight passenger cars were acquired at the same time from abandoned lines in Ohio and New York.

At war's end, the decline of the interurban railways resumed all too quickly. Maine's Aroostook Valley Railroad, the Hershey Transit Company in Pennsylvania, West Virginia's little Tri-City Traction, and the long Salt Lake & Utah had all been abandoned entirely or given up passenger operation before the end of 1946. Two of the Oklahoma Railway's interurban routes went the same year, and the company's last interurban line—to Norman—went the following year. A half dozen principal casualties in 1947 included the Utah Idaho Central, and the last interurbans in Georgia, West Virginia, and New York. New Jersey's last interurban—the Atlantic City & Shore—and the Texas Electric were both abandoned in 1948, the latter after a serious head-on collision that injured some 30 passengers. Over the next two years the Baltimore & Annapolis, the Des Moines & Central Iowa and the Denver & Intermountain all gave up passenger service. In 1950, after traffic had fallen to scarcely half of its peak wartime level, even the great Pacific Electric made major abandonments of rail passenger service; by year's end only five PE rail routes continued to operate.

But even amidst this collapse of much of what was left of the industry, there was still some occasional good news. The Chicago, Aurora & Elgin, whose plans for new cars had been delayed by the war, received ten new steel passenger cars from St. Louis Car in 1946. The neighboring South Shore Line continued its wartime program for lengthening passenger cars, and by 1951 had completed work on 36 cars. All of the post-war rebuilt cars included air conditioning, new seating, lengthened "picture" windows, and other improvements, and some of the wartime rebuilds were returned to the shops for similar treatment, giving the line a thoroughly modernized 18-car fleet that was adequate to operate all of its long-haul schedules. Still another major South Shore improvement was carried out during 1954-56, when a five-mile, grade-separated bypass was built around East Chicago, Indiana, taking South Shore freight and passenger trains off one of the city's principal streets. In 1950 the North Shore, the third of the former Insull interurbans at Chicago, began a *Silverliner* modernization program for its standard steel car fleet that eventually reached a total of 30 rebuilt cars.

Two interurbans bought new PCC, or PCC-type, cars for their suburban services during the post-war period. In 1949 the Philadelphia Suburban Transportation Company took delivery of 14 double-end, multiple unit cars for its suburban routes out of 69th Street Terminal in Upper Darby. While similar to PCC cars in appearance and other features, the Red Arrow cars were fitted with more conventional equalized trucks capable of 70 m.p.h. speeds. The same year, the Illinois Terminal received eight similar double-end, multiple unit PCCs for its suburban services between St. Louis and Granite City, Illinois.

The most extraordinary interurban equipment development in the immediate post-war period, however, was the Illinois Terminal Railroad's ill-fated venture in streamlined trains. Encouraged by a wartime interurban passenger traffic that had reached a 1945 peak of 8.6 million passengers, IT announced early in 1946 a million dollar order with St. Louis Car Company for eight streamlined cars that would make up three new trains for high-speed limited train service on its principal lines. Named the *City of Decatur*, the *Fort Crevecoeur*, and the *Mound City*, the new trains entered service in 1948-49 on IT's St. Louis-Decatur and St. Louis-Peoria runs. Accommodations on each train included deluxe air conditioned coaches and a dining-parlor-observation car.

For most of the industry, however, the steady decline of the post-war years continued. Milwaukee's last interurban routes to the west had been sold to a new operator, the Milwaukee Rapid Transit

& Speedrail Company, in 1949 and reequipped with used Cincinnati curved side lightweight cars. A promising recovery ended abruptly with a disastrous head-on collision of two railfan excursion trains that took ten lives in September 1950. The company went bankrupt soon afterward, and abandonment came the following year. The same year the Salt Lake, Garfield & Western gave up electric passenger operation, and the Lehigh Valley Transit abandoned its long Allentown-Norristown "Liberty Bell Limited" route, one again putting the line's former C&LE and Indiana lightweight, high-speed cars out of work, this time for good. In 1952, Iowa's Charles City Western, the Bamberger Railroad, and three Pennsylvania lines—the West Penn, the Pittsburgh Railways, and the Lackawanna & Wyoming Valley—were either abandoned outright or gave up their interurban passenger operations. The balance of the surviving C&LE and Indiana cars were out of service the following year, when the Cedar Rapids & Iowa City shut down its electric passenger service.

Abandonments of the few remaining interurban passenger lines continued through the balance of the 1950's. The last Hagerstown & Frederick line, and the Philadelphia Suburban's long West Chester line, closed in 1954. The two Canadian Pacific electrics in Ontario and the Sand Springs Railway abandoned passenger operations in 1955. The North Shore closed its Shore Line suburban route the same year. Iowa's last two passenger electrics, the Fort Dodge Line and the Waterloo, Cedar Falls & Northern, ended service in 1955 and 1956. Despite the introduction of its splendid streamliners, Illinois Terminal's interurban passenger traffic had largely vanished by the early 1950's, and the road gave up its last interurban passenger service early in 1956. There were no prospective buyers for the costly streamliners, and some years later they were cut up for scrap. IT's suburban service at St. Louis lasted for another two years, before it, too, was abandoned.

Canada's London & Port Stanley abandoned passenger operation in 1957. Far more significant, however, was the closure in the same year of the first of the three great Insull interurbans at Chicago. Traffic on the Chicago, Aurora & Elgin had declined drastically after 1954, when expressway construction had cut off the line's direct access to the Chicago Loop, and the line was shut down in July 1957. The British Columbia Electric Railway and Portland's Oregon City route, the very first interurban line, closed in 1958. Canada's last two interurban passenger operations, Canadian National's Quebec interurban and the Niagara, St. Catharines & Toronto, shut down early in 1959, and after that there wasn't much of anything left.

The Pacific Electric's surviving rail passenger services had been sold in 1954 to bus operator Metropolitan Coach Lines, and, a few years later, to a new Metropolitan Transit Authority. All but one of the former PE rail routes had been abandoned by the end of the decade, and the last segment of what was once the world's greatest interurban railway, the Los Angeles-Long Beach route, was closed in 1961.

The interurban era truly came to an end early on the cold, snowy morning of January 21, 1963, when the last train of the last traditional American interurban—the North Shore Line—ended its run at 2:55 a.m. at the line's Milwaukee terminal. Despite a spirited struggle to survive in a changed world, even the great North Shore had proved unable to make it.

Although the North Shore was an interurban electric railway on a much grander scale than most, the reasons for its ultimate failure were representative of those that affected almost all interurbans. Perhaps, for that reason, they warrant a brief review.

Like most interurbans, the North Shore was always primarily a passenger carrier, dependent upon both a substantial commuter traffic from the suburban communities north of Chicago and on inter-city traffic between Chicago, Milwaukee, and the intermediate cities along the Lake Michigan shore. From the late 1920's onward, that traffic had been in a long-term decline as improved roads and advancing automobile ownership and usage steadily eroded the interurban's traffic base. Traffic rebounded to record levels during the World War II years, before resuming an even more rapid decline at war's end. From a 1945 peak of nearly 28 million passengers, North Shore traffic had dropped to less than 10 million within only three years. As traffic continued to fall, the railroad found it increasingly difficult to operate at a profit. The constantly tighter squeeze between wages and other operating costs and operating revenues was aggravated by an inherently low productivity of labor, plant and equipment in what had become increasingly a commuter operation. From 1947 onward the North Shore reported annual net losses that by 1958 had reached a total of well over $4 million.

Construction of new highways assured a continued loss of traffic to private automobiles. The opening of a new expressway into the Chicago Loop in 1960, for example, cost the North Shore more than 40,000 passengers a month. In the road's final years, annual passenger traffic had dropped to scarcely four million.

Like many interurbans, the North Shore had made a determined effort to augment its passenger revenues with freight traffic. Despite a well-developed merchandise dispatch service, an innovative early piggyback service, or aggressive efforts to develop overhead traffic, the North Shore was never able to develop the solid base of freight traffic that it needed for long-term survival. Freight revenues never accounted for much more than a quarter of total earnings, and in the line's last years freight earnings represented only about 15 percent of total North Shore income.

As one after another of the surviving interurbans gave up passenger service in the post-war period, many of them continued to operate as electrically-powered freight railroads. Some converted to diesel operation almost immediately, and almost all of them did so sooner or later. Over time, many of these freight-only survivors have lost their identity by incorporation into the main line railroad system. The Pacific Electric Railway, for example, continued to operate for a time as a diesel-powered freight feeder to the parent Southern Pacific Company, and was then merged into the SP altogether. Much the same thing happened to the portions of the Sacramento Northern Railroad retained for freight service, which were eventually merged into SN's parent Western Pacific. Soon after interurban passenger service ended on Illinois Terminal in 1956, the line was acquired by ten steam railroads. Gradually, much of the one-time interurban's track was torn up and traffic shifted to parallel lines of its new owners. Finally, in 1981, the IT was acquired by the Norfolk & Western and merged with its new owner.

If the traditional interurban railway was gone by 1963, there were still a few surviving passenger-carrying electric railways that retained much of the character of their interurban origins. At Philadelphia, the Media and Sharon Hill suburban routes of the Philadelphia Suburban Traction Company, as well as the high-speed Norristown route of the Philadelphia & Western continued to operate. The P&W had been merged into the PSTCo "Red Arrow" system in 1954, and the lines became part of the regional Southeastern Pennsylvania Transportation Authority (SEPTA) in 1970.

The premier survivor from the interurban era, however, was the Chicago South Shore & South Bend, the one-time Insull interurban that had evolved into what was essentially a heavy freight and electrified commuter railroad.

Both of these surviving systems have been the scene of some interesting equipment developments. In 1963, in what is likely to have been the last used equipment move between two interurbans, the Red Arrow Lines acquired the two North Shore Line *Electroliners* for continued service on the former P&W high-speed line to Norristown. Red Arrow shops extensively overhauled and refurbished the two trains as the *Liberty Liners* "Valley Forge" and "Independence Hall," and the trains entered regular service early in 1964, offering tavern-lounge section breakfast and beverage service to rush hour passengers. The trains continued to operate opposite the line's celebrated Brill "Bullet" cars until 1976, when they were retired for a second time, this time to trolley museums.

SEPTA's former Red Arrow suburban routes to Media and Sharon Hill got a complete new outfitting of equipment in 1982, when 29 light rail vehicles from Japan's Kawasaki Heavy Industries went into service on the two lines. The new cars were a double-end version of the 112 new Kawasaki cars supplied for SEPTA's West Philadelphia subway-surface routes.

Supplemented by even older "Strafford" cars built by J.G. Brill during 1924-1929, and—since 1987—by ex-Chicago Transit Authority PCC-type rapid transit cars, the famed Brill Bullet cars have continued to operate through the 1980's in high-speed service over SEPTA's ex-P&W high-speed line to Norristown. Soon after the end of the decade, however, the splendid aerodynamic interurbans are scheduled for replacement by a fleet of 26 new cars that will represent as advanced a car in their time as the Bullets did in theirs. SEPTA's equipment engineers have specified a new car with such features as stainless steel carbody construction, air conditioning, and a three-phase A.C. induction motor drive, having microprocessor control of propulsion, spin-slide detection, and braking. Braking will be dynamic braking with a regenerative capability, supplemented by disc brakes, while the cars' outside frame trucks will have such features as rubber and air bag suspension, and a limited steering capability. An order placed with a joint venture of Amtrak and Sweden's ASEA late in 1987 should see a pilot car in test operation during the winter of 1989-90, with the full 26-car fleet in service by 1991.

The surviving South Shore Line, too, got a new passenger equipment outfitting in the early 1980's, but only after years of uncertainty about the future of any South Shore passenger service at all. The line had reported a passenger deficit for every year from 1951 onward; by 1969 the annual loss had reached $750,000 and was enough, in some years, to more than offset freight earnings. South Shore efforts to gain public support for its passenger service under provisions of the Urban Mass Transportation Assistance Act began in the late 1960's. Some help for the Illinois end of its passenger operations came in 1973, but it was not until a threat of total passenger service abandonment in late 1976 that Indiana finally acted. Formation of the Northern Indiana Commuter Transportation District provided a local agency through which assistance funding was channeled beginning in 1978. Within a few years NICTD was able to put together a major capital improvement program for South Shore passenger service that included passenger station improvements, expanded power supply, improved shop facilities, and 44 new passenger cars. Delivered by Japan's Sumitomo Corporation during 1982-83, the new cars were 85-foot, stainless steel coaches that bore a much closer resemblance to modern commuter railroad rolling stock than they did to the traditional interurbans they replaced. Even with its new rolling stock, and a steadily growing level of ridership, the South Shore's future as a passenger carrier has remained clouded, largely because of uncertainties in the continuing availability of the public funding needed to sustain the service.

While it was going through the long struggle to obtain new passenger equipment, the South Shore phased out its electric freight operation. Soon after the Chesapeake & Ohio had acquired control of the South Shore in 1967, the parent road began supplementing the line's electric motive power with diesels. Finally, delivery of ten brand new GP38-2 units from GM's Electro Motive Division early in 1981 permitted South Shore to drop the pantograph on its last electric locomotive.

Outside the continental U.S. still another North American interurban continued to operate an electric intercity passenger service. This was the one-time Hershey Cuban Railway, which was nationalized as part of the Ferrocarriles de Cuba in 1960. Although newer equipment has been acquired by the Cuban line, recent reports indicate that at least some of the Hershey's original early-1920's Brill and Wason interurbans are still at work.

If the South Shore and SEPTA's former Red Arrow suburban lines at Philadelphia were the only direct U.S. descendants from the interurban era, there were sometimes some remarkable parallels between the new rapid transit or light rail systems and the interurbans of an earlier time.

In the San Francisco Bay Area, for example, the Bay Area Rapid Transit District's Concord route crossed the Oakland Hills to serve suburban communities once reached by Sacramento Northern interurbans, while BART's East Bay lines reached many destinations once located along the routes of SP's Interurban Electric and the Key System.

At Portland, Oregon, the new Banfield light rail route reached its Gresham terminal over track relaid on the roadbed of an old Portland Traction interurban line. At Los Angeles, a new county-wide rapid transit and light rail system was taking shape which would ultimately parallel many of the principal routes of the old Pacific Electric Railway. Indeed, the system's first light rail route now under construction between Los Angeles and Long Beach follows the route of the old PE interurban line to Long Beach with but little deviation. At still other locations, such as San Diego, San Jose, and Sacramento, the new light rail lines were reaching out to suburban communities on long routes not unlike interurbans.

Among proposed light rail routes there were still others that came even closer to a sort of "new generation" interurban. Late in

1987 Maryland Governor William Schaefer announced plans for a light rail line from Baltimore that would closely parallel the old Baltimore & Annapolis to the Baltimore-Washington International Airport and Glen Burnie, with a possible later extension to Annapolis. In Virginia, there was a proposal to link Norfolk and Virginia Beach with a new light rail route. Minneapolis had a proposal for a long line to Excelsior, on the shores of Lake Minnetonka. A 1986 proposal by San Antonio Mayor Henry Cisneros suggested study of a 110-mile regional light rail system that would include a 79-mile line to Austin. More recently, early

in 1987, Oklahoma's Department of Transportation was seeking federal funds for study of a 200-mile light rail system that would include long routes linking Tulsa with Oklahoma City and Bartlesville, as well as shorter urban transit rail routes at Tulsa and Oklahoma City. Late in 1987 the California Transportation Commission proposed that San Francisco-San Jose commuter trains be replaced by high-speed trolleys—interurbans if you will—that could operate directly into the Santa Clara County light rail system.

Perhaps the interurban era wasn't entirely over after all!

The passing of the interurban industry was evidenced, in part, by the virtual lack of investment in new equipment. On the next few pages, we illustrate all the new rolling stock purchased by the industry. In total, the industry received 64 intercity passenger cars, 67 suburban cars and 3 freight locomotives. ABOVE: On Sunday, November 7, 1948, the first run of the eight units which comprised the Illinois Terminal streamliners. Train number 91 stops at Illiopolis, Illinois, a town between Decatur and Springfield. *(WCJ)* ADJACENT PAGE TOP LEFT: On Saturday, February 8, 1941, one of the two Electroliners of the Chicago, North Shore & Milwaukee pauses at South Upton Junction. This was an inspection trip for CERA. On the following day, these two trains entered service. *(RVM)* TOP RIGHT: On December 16, 1945, the Chicago Aurora & Elgin operated an inspection trip for CERA in its new 450-series cars. The

10 new cars entered service on December 10. Cars 453 and 451 are at Ferry Road on the Aurora Branch. BOTTOM LEFT: In 1949, the Chicago South Shore & South Bend received three of the electric locomotives that had been built by General Electric for Russia. On November 6, 1949, locomotive 803 leads a CERA inspection trip 53 out of Burnham Yard to South Bend. *(Both photos WCJ)* BOTTOM RIGHT: By far the largest order for 44 new cars for the Chicago South Shore & South Bend. These cars' bodies were fabricated by Nippon Sharyo Seizo Kaisha Ltd. and shipped to the United States. Motors, control equipment and brakes were installed in the U.S. These cars were delivered in 1982 and 1983. They entered revenue service on November 22, 1982. On July 13, 1983, car 7 and friend have arrived at South Bend as train 25 from Chicago. In a few minutes, these cars will deadhead to Michigan City. *(WDM)*

For lines that served nearby suburban areas, the interurban companies turned to streetcar technology for the three new orders that were delivered in the 50-year period of this study. TOP LEFT: On November 24, 1940, the Pacific Electric placed an order for 30 PCC cars built by Pullman-Standard. Car 5007 is inbound from Glendale-Burbank crossing the Fletcher Drive trestle en route to Los Angeles in 1954. *(WDM)* TOP RIGHT: In November, 1949, the Illinois Terminal placed in service eight PCC cars from St. Louis Car Co. Until June, 1958, these cars served between St. Louis, Missouri, and Granite City, Illinois. On July 3, 1950, car 452 is turning from State St. onto 18th Street in Granite City. When these cars stopped running, the Illinois Terminal exited the passenger business. *(WCJ)* LEFT: Philadelphia's SEPTA needed to replace its rolling stock in the 1980's. The suburban routes to Media and Sharon Hill were reequipped in 1982 with 29 light rail vehicles built by Kawasaki Heavy Industries. Car 117 is westbound at Drexel Hill Junction en route to Media on December 9, 1985. *(WDM)*

New England interurbans were more like light rail lines. Essentially, they provided local and suburban service. ABOVE: The Springfield Terminal Railroad is known to virtually all railroaders and rail fans in the late 1980's. This is the railroad corporate structure and dominant union contract that was used by the management of Guilford Transportation to operate, under trackage rights agreements, the Maine Central, Boston & Maine and parts of the Delaware & Hudson. In the more tranquil days, car 10 is on the main line below Springfield, Vermont, on February 23, 1941. *(Stanley Hauck photo, C. L. Siebert, Jr. Collection)* RIGHT: Cars in New England were typically the suburban type and designed for rugged weather. On a snowy April 21, 1940, Androscoggin and Kennebec Railway car 188 is at the end of the line at Lake Cove, Maine. *(C. L. Siebert photo)*

In Canada, the interurbans were built to steam-road standards in part because of ownership by the major railroads from an early date. TOP: On July 4, 1946, Lake Erie & Northern car 955 is on a Grand River Railway run from Kitchener to Galt, Ontario, while Kitchener-Waterloo car 40 is at Kitchener Junction to meet the interurban. Both the LE&N and the GRR were owned by the Canadian Pacific Railway. The Canadian National Railways owned numerous interurbans, including the Montreal and Southern Counties and, after 1951, the Quebec Railway Light and Power Co. interurban operations. ABOVE: M&SC 501 is at Granby in June 18, 1947. *(Two photos WCJ)* RIGHT: QRL&P 451 is laying over between trips at Montmorency Falls. *(WDM)*

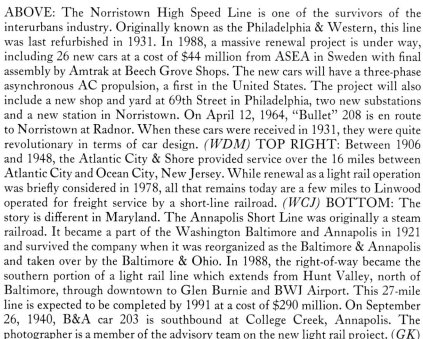

ABOVE: The Norristown High Speed Line is one of the survivors of the interurbans industry. Originally known as the Philadelphia & Western, this line was last refurbished in 1931. In 1988, a massive renewal project is under way, including 26 new cars at a cost of $44 million from ASEA in Sweden with final assembly by Amtrak at Beech Grove Shops. The new cars will have a three-phase asynchronous AC propulsion, a first in the United States. The project will also include a new shop and yard at 69th Street in Philadelphia, two new substations and a new station in Norristown. On April 12, 1964, "Bullet" 208 is en route to Norristown at Radnor. When these cars were received in 1931, they were quite revolutionary in terms of car design. *(WDM)* TOP RIGHT: Between 1906 and 1948, the Atlantic City & Shore provided service over the 16 miles between Atlantic City and Ocean City, New Jersey. While renewal as a light rail operation was briefly considered in 1978, all that remains today are a few miles to Linwood operated for freight service by a short-line railroad. *(WCJ)* BOTTOM: The story is different in Maryland. The Annapolis Short Line was originally a steam railroad. It became a part of the Washington Baltimore and Annapolis in 1921 and survived the company when it was reorganized as the Baltimore & Annapolis and taken over by the Baltimore & Ohio. In 1988, the right-of-way became the southern portion of a light rail line which extends from Hunt Valley, north of Baltimore, through downtown to Glen Burnie and BWI Airport. This 27-mile line is expected to be completed by 1991 at a cost of $290 million. On September 26, 1940, B&A car 203 is southbound at College Creek, Annapolis. The photographer is a member of the advisory team on the new light rail project. *(GK)*

The West Penn Railways System included the operations of the West Penn, Wheeling (West Virginia) Traction Company and the Monongahela West Penn Public Service Company *(MWP)*, which principally operated in West Virginia. This complex in southwestern Pennsylvania, West Virginia and along a portion of the Ohio River in Ohio was owned by American Water Works and Electric Company. American Water Works had extensive public utility holdings, including the Hagerstown and Frederick, an interurban which operated in Maryland. ABOVE: The West Penn served the Coke Region southeast of Pittsburgh with a network of lines extending from connections with Pittsburgh Railways at Trafford and McKeesport via Greensburg, Connellsville and Uniontown to Fairchance and Brownsville. At one time, half-hourly service was offered between Uniontown and Greensburg. On September 9, 1946, car 706 was in Uniontown. Rail service into Uniontown survived until August 9, 1952. *(WCJ)* LEFT: As a result of the Public Utility Holding Company Act, American Water Works sold, in 1944, the two lines (Fairmont-Clarksburg-Weston and Parkersburg-Marietta, Ohio) of MWP to a free-standing company named City Lines of West Virginia. Rail service lasted only three years under this ownership. On September 8, 1946, City Lines car 228 is in Fairmont.*(GK)*.

By 1938, interurban operations were virtually gone from the State of Ohio and the end was in sight for the Indiana Railroad System's rail operations, as the service was being converted to buses. Early in CERA's history, there were trips over the IR but that was to come to an end with the cessation of rail operations on January 19, 1941. A single round trip daily survived between Indianapolis and Seymour. This so-called "franchise run" resulted from a long-term lease executed by a predecessor company. RIGHT: Car 76 is holding down this run on a summer day in 1941. This operation came to an abrupt end on September 8, 1941, when sister car 78 met line car 772 in a head-on collision south of Columbus, Indiana. *(WCJ)* BELOW: Meanwhile, in Illinois, passenger operations on the Illinois Terminal continued, a tribute to A. P. Titus, the railroad's president. To fulfill its pledge for improved service and while awaiting delivery of the Streamliners (see page 53), the railroad modernized some of its best interurban cars and distinguished them with this "whisker" stripe and assigned them to the Limiteds. On May 31, 1948, car 285 is leading the Illmo Limited through Granite City, Illinois, at 22nd and Washington Streets. Passenger service ended on March 3, 1956, following a series of cutbacks. *(Gordon E. Lloyd Photo)*

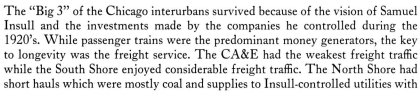

The "Big 3" of the Chicago interurbans survived because of the vision of Samuel Insull and the investments made by the companies he controlled during the 1920's. While passenger trains were the predominant money generators, the key to longevity was the freight service. The CA&E had the weakest freight traffic while the South Shore enjoyed considerable freight traffic. The North Shore had short hauls which were mostly coal and supplies to Insull-controlled utilities with some interchange traffic. The zeal with which Insull pursued coal traffic is evidenced by routing of coal where the Chicago & Northwestern would interchange coal to the North Shore only to have the North Shore give it back to the C&NW for delivery to the generating stations. TOP LEFT: The Chicago Aurora & Elgin was the first to go. On August 17, 1946, car 413 is leading a rush-hour train westbound past the Home Avenue station. This location is now

in the middle of the Eisenhower Expressway between Harlem and Des Plaines Avenues near where the present day Congress rapid transit line crosses over the expressway. On September 20, 1953, passenger service was cut back from Wells Street terminal to Des Plaines Avenue, Forest Park, and abandoned completely on July 3, 1957. Freight service ended on July 9, 1959. *(WCJ)* TOP RIGHT: North Shore became a heavy commuter hauler but revenues were not sufficient to replace its aging equipment, particularly after the Edens Expressway opened and C&NW modernized its commuter service. Service over the Shore Line through the posh North Shore suburbs ended on July 25, 1955, and complete abandonment followed on January 21, 1963. On September 16, 1947, this four-car train is northbound at Layton Avenue in Milwaukee. BOTTOM: While the Insull-era cars of the South Shore rolled their last miles in 1983, the passenger service continues in 1988 but only after substantial public investments and subsidies plus a series of financial crises that have threatened to terminate the service. This four-car train is in the Calumet Harbor area alongside 130th Street in Chicago on June 7, 1948. *(Two photos RVM)* ABOVE: North Shore 453 plus two other "pups" and one of the "battery" motors are ready to depart Pettibone Yard, North Chicago, for the EJ&E interchange at Roundout with 35 loads on January 1, 1958. *(WDM)* LEFT: South Shore's 900's began life on the Illinois Central. They came to the South Shore in 1941. On April 30, 1949, they are westbound at Wagner Siding near Gary. *(Krambles Collection)*

LEFT: Segments of the three major interurban lines operated by The Milwaukee Electric Railway & Light Company *(TM)* lasted a relatively long time. In September, 1947, one of TM's duplex units is crossing over the Milwaukee Road at the Mequon Stone Quarry south of Cedarsburg, Wisconsin. Interurban operations ended in Milwaukee on June 30, 1951, following a successor company entering trusteeship in November, 1950. BELOW LEFT: Iowa was the land of "steam road trolleys" and notable bridges. The Fort Dodge Des Moines & Southern replaced a wooden trestle on this site with this huge steel structure at a cost of only $90,000. The structure opened for traffic on November 17, 1912, and is still used in 1988 by a tourist railway. On July 13, 1940, car 62 is crossing the trestle which was the most imposing of a series of bridges on the line. Passenger service ended on August 31, 1955. Freight service continued for about 15 years thereafter. *(Two photos WCJ)* BELOW RIGHT: Multiple crossings of Cedar River confronted the Waterloo Cedar Falls & Northern with civil engineering challenges. Three concrete arch bridges were constructed, one near downtown Waterloo on the Cedar Falls line, one just south of Waterloo near Elk Run and this bridge south of La Porte City, about one third of the way to Cedar Rapids. One of WCF&N's observation cars is carrying members of CERA on an inspection trip. *(Wallace Rogers photo, WCJ Collection)* FACING PAGE TOP: One survivor of the Iowa interurbans is the Cedar Rapids & Iowa City, more commonly known as the Crandic. In 1988, diesel-powered freight service continues for the line's only owner since incorporation in 1903, Iowa Electric. In 1939, Crandic purchased six of these high-speed interurban cars from the Cincinnati & Lake Erie. Car 116 is preparing for its maiden run on the Crandic, still in its C&LE livery. This trip on May 28, 1939, was a special trip to celebrate CERA's first anniversary. Crandic's master mechanic, John Munson, was at the

controls. Passenger service was discontinued on October 15, 1953. Diesel freight service remains very profitable in 1988. *(GK)* Iowa has the distinction of having the longest continuous electric operation. Electric railway service began on the Mason City & Clear Lake in 1897. Since late 1987, the railroad has been known as the Iowa Traction Railroad. As of 1988, the MC&CL and its successors have joined to provide 91 years of electric railway service, the longest continuous electric operation of an interurban railway in the United States. BELOW: The Texas Electric Railway provided interurban service from Dallas north to Sherman and Denison and south on two lines, one to Corsicana and the other to Waco. At one time, other companies provided service from Dallas to Ft. Worth, Denton and Terrill. On Thursday, September 11, 1941, Train 11, car 319, holds the main track at George Siding, just south of Howe, Texas, on the Denison Division for its meeting with Train IV. Howe is the first town south of Sherman. Texas Electric's rail operations ended on December 31, 1948. Buses took over the following day. *(John F. Humiston photo)* Much of the area surrounding Dallas is now an urban metroplex. In 1988, the return of rail service is being debated by Dallas area citizens.

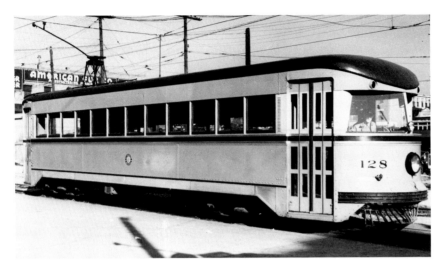

Four companies provided interurban service in Utah. TOP LEFT: Bamberger Railroad connected Salt Lake City and Ogden with frequent service. Car 128, shown at Salt Lake on September 29, 1939, is one of five high-speed lightweight "Bullet" cars built by Brill in 1932 for the Fonda, Johnstown & Gloversville (New York) Railroad. They came to Utah in 1939 and were the only truly modern interurban cars in the West. Passenger service on the Bamberger ended on September 7, 1952. *(GK)* TOP RIGHT: The Salt Lake, Garfield & Western connected Salt Lake City with the Saltair Pavilion over an arrow-straight route. Built as a steam railroad in 1893, electric operations commenced on August 4, 1919. On August 16, 1951, diesels took over hauling trains to the Pavilion. On August 5, 1937, car 504 is trained with two of the Saltair's famous open cars at Salt Lake City. BOTTOM LEFT: The Salt Lake & Utah Railroad, commonly known as "The Orem Line," connected Salt Lake City with Provo and Payson. Interurbans in Utah were family affairs, with the Bamberger and Orem families constructing and operating their respective railways. Car 609 is at Provo on September 29, 1939. Never financially sound, the Orem's operation ended with only five days' notice on February 28, 1946, with the company in receivership. BOTTOM RIGHT: To the north, the Utah Idaho Central served

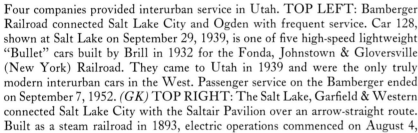

the area from Ogden via Logan, Utah, to Preston, Idaho, a territory that was sparsely populated. Train service was never frequent. On September 28, 1939, car 509 is on the rear of one of the few daily through trains. Almost one year to the date following the Orem, UIC's rail passenger operations ended, in receivership, on February 15, 1947, with two days' notice. Freight service ended on February 28, 1947, exactly one year after the Orem shutdown. In both cases, the same receiver, S. J. Quinney, petitioned the same Federal judge, Tillman D. Johnson, to shut down the interurbans. *(Three photos WCJ)* THIS PAGE: Portland Traction 4018, a former Pacific Electric Hollywood car, is southbound at Milwaukie, Oregon, on October 12, 1955. At this time, Portland Traction

was operating a virtual museum of second-hand equipment. Portland Traction's predecessor was among America's first interurbans, with service beginning on February 16, 1893. Passenger service ended abruptly on January 25, 1958, with the company still embroiled in controversy with the regulatory agencies after the county supervisors barred the railcars from using the Willamette River bridge and entry into downtown Portland. Things are much different in the 1980's. In September, 1986, service began on Portland's light rail system, known as Metropolitan Area eXpress—MAX, for short. MAX's new Bombardier-built Light Rail Vehicles use this same Willamette River bridge and portions of the Portland Traction's right-of-way on the 15-mile trip to Gresham. *(WDM)*

The Sacramento Northern Railway had something for everybody, including mountains, high-speed flatlands, a ferry boat ride en route, parlor car accommodations in open observation cars and the longest interurban route—183 miles from Chico via Sacramento to Oakland—which in its final years extended across the Oakland Bay Bridge to the Ferry Building in San Francisco. Always a heavy freight hauler and owned from its early years by the Western Pacific Railroad, it was much like the Illinois Terminal, more of a steam road in terms of operations than an interurban. The SN was really two railroads, the Northern Electric, from Sacramento north to Chico, and the Oakland, Antioch & Eastern from

Sacramento and Pittsburg through Concord, Walnut Creek and Lafayette to Oakland. BART's Concord route serves this same territory and occupies portions of SN's right-of-way in Walnut Creek and Concord. Proposed extensions to BART will virtually replicate the OA&E south of Suisun Bay. ABOVE: Extra 1009 meets another train at Pinehurst, in the Oakland Hills south of Lafayette on June 18, 1939. FACING PAGE TOP RIGHT: The "Bidwell" shown here at Key System's Emeryville (Oakland) yard on February 23, 1938, was one of four parlor cars on the SN. *(Two photos Charles Smallwood, Krambles Collection)* BOTTOM RIGHT: While always important on the OA&E,

freight service became increasingly meaningful on the north end as well. However, to the end, freight trains never operated through Sacramento. On January 30, 1951, motor 660 is descending into Oakland. Final operation of mainline electric freight occurred between Oakland and West Lafayette on March 1, 1957. *(WDM)* BOTTOM LEFT: The north end was built with third rail and the south end with overhead with both pantographs and trolley poles being used for power collection. In later years, south end cars were preferred because of their larger motors. On September 24, 1939, at approximately 6:00 p.m., Mr. R. Sax is detaching the third rail shoes from southbound train number 11 at Sacramento Union Depot. *(GK)* TOP RIGHT: Complete with lunchroom, the gasoline-powered ferry "Ramon" bridged the Suisun Bay tidal basin. This was literally the interurban at sea. On June 29, 1940, train number 2 is crossing the bay heading for Mallard on the south side of the bay. Chipps was the landing on the north side. *(John F. Humiston photo)*

Freight service was meaningful to all California interurbans. That was due in large measure to the steam roads owning the interurbans. The Southern Pacific owned 100% of the Pacific Electric and one-third of Central California Traction Company. Ownership of the CCT was shared equally with the Western Pacific and Santa Fe. CCT connected Stockton to Sacramento over a 53-mile mainline with a branch to Lodi. Its principal reason for existence was to feed freight to its owners. Passenger service ended in 1933. ABOVE: Motor 6 with help from a friend in the rear is moving a fruitblock to the connections. (GK) RIGHT: Pacific Electric operated a freight service, with steam, electric motors and diesels, and an express and railway post office service, with a fleet of 78 box motors in the 1400 class, until abandonment of this service on November 15, 1952. This service started in the 1890's with two cars traveling between Los Angeles and Pasadena. On January 1, 1951, motor 1447, which started life on the Portland, Eugene & Eastern in Oregon, is at Monrovia Station on the Glendora line. *(WDM)* Carload freight service on the Pacific Electric was absorbed by its parent, Southern Pacific, along with the railroad itself. In 1988, some Pacific Electric track exists but the traffic generally moves on paralleling S.P. trackage.

The diversity of Pacific Electric's operation is documented on this page; interurban, suburban and streetcar service was provided over approximately 700 route miles in the Los Angeles area. Virtually every area was served by the "Red Cars." The center of operations was at 6th and Main, a building which stands in 1988, and the former station area inside the building is now a parking lot. In brighter days, car 1024 is on the rear of an Alhambra-Temple City train that is departing in July, 1941, as it moves north on Main Street. Coming south is a Pasadena train. Service beyond Alhambra to Temple City was abandoned in December, 1941, and to Alhambra in 1948. Rail service to Pasadena ended on September 30, 1951. (GK) BOTTOM RIGHT: "Hollywood car" 5105 is approaching Cahuenga Pass en route from North Sherman Way in Van Nuys to Los Angeles on September 24, 1950. The route through Cahuenga Pass is now covered over by the Hollywood Freeway. (WDM) BOTTOM LEFT: Car 111 is providing service on August 20, 1948, on the Echo Park Avenue line, which started at 11th and Hill Streets and operated via Sunset Boulevard and Echo Park Avenue to Cerro Gordo Street, a distance of 4.56 miles. This line was converted to a bus operation on October 1, 1950. (Thomas H. Desnoyers photo, Krambles Collection)

ABOVE: On September 19, 1948, car 1245 is near Los Angeles Union Passenger Terminal on a run to Baldwin Park, which was the "cutback" point on the San Bernardino line. The train is approaching the Macy Street trackage, which became the Achilles heel of the Northern District. The right-of-way was needed for freeway construction. *(Thomas H. Desnoyers photo, Krambles Collection)* TOP RIGHT: El Molino was the junction point of the Pasadena Oak Knoll line which turned to the left and the line to Glendora and the branch to Sierra Madre. Believe it or not, this junction is in the middle of Huntington Boulevard in San Marino. In 1988, it is covered over by the roadway. On January 4, 1951, car 1134 is on the rear of a three-car Santa Anita Racetrack Special. Rail service to Pasadena Via Oak Knoll was abandoned in October, 1950, and to Sierra Madre on December 28, 1950. Passenger service to Monrovia-Glendora terminated on September, 1951; however, freight service, via an S.P. branch between Arcadia and Glendora, ran until 1959. *(WDM)* BOTTOM RIGHT: Car 317 started its career on the Northwestern Pacific on the Marin Peninsula north of San Francisco. In the 1950's, the car is northbound on a Los Angeles Limited, crossing the S.P. San Pedro line at Dominquez Junction. Dominquez Junction is the point where the line to San Pedro separated from the Long Beach line. Passenger service to San Pedro ended on December 8, 1958. Pacific Electric was chartered in 1901

by Henry Huntington, and the Long Beach line was the first line opened by Huntington on July 4, 1902. It was the last line operated by Pacific Electric's successor, Los Angeles Metropolitan Transit Authority, when rail passenger service was discontinued on April 9, 1961. In 1988, construction is well advanced on the new Long Beach light rail line, which is scheduled to open in 1990. At this site, a bridge will carry the Long Beach light rail line over the Southern Pacific railroad and Alemeda Street. Fully 90% of the Long Beach light rail line will traverse the right-of-way of Pacific Electric's Long Beach Line. Some of the same rails which carried the Pacific Electric trains were removed in 1987 and 1988 as a part of the light rail construction. *(WDM)* ABOVE: One of the more famous of Pacific Electric's lines was the Venice Short Line, which operated from the Hill Street Station, near 4th and Hill Streets in downtown Los Angeles, via a median strip in Venice Boulevard through Culver City to the beaches at Venice and up the "trolley way" to Santa Monica, a 17-mile trip in total. The line was an extraordinary operation for Pacific Electric as it hauled huge crowds to the beaches and thousands of kids to school. On this bright day in the 1940's, car

989, an ex-Los Angeles Pacific Railway car which served this line throughout its and the line's existence, is testimony to one of Pacific Electric's basic problems—virtually no replacement of rolling stock after the 1920's. Service on the Venice Short Line was converted to buses on September 17, 1950 *(GK)* The renaissance of rail service in Los Angeles is not limited to the Long Beach line. Another light rail line is being constructed in the Century Freeway between Norwalk and El Segundo, with possible extensions to Los Angeles International Airport and/or Redondo Beach. Meanwhile, the residents of Pasadena are actively seeking a light rail line. In downtown Los Angeles, $1.25 billion is being spent on the 4-mile "starter line" between Los Angeles Union Passenger Terminal through downtown and into the Wilshire corridor. There are plans to extend this into a 40-mile system. Discussions regarding commuter rail are also in process as the freeway system is reaching the saturation point and urban planners are looking back to rail as the solution to moving people. The more things change, the more they stay the same. Los Angeles may again emerge as a passenger rail center as residents continually ask, "Why did we get rid of the 'Red Cars'?"

CHAPTER 3

RAPID TRANSIT IN NORTH AMERICA

Throughout the first half of the 20th century subways or elevated railways had been developed in only the very largest North American cities – New York, Boston, Philadelphia, and Chicago. Compared on the basis of such measures as rolling stock ownership or track mileage, these rapid transit systems were far exceeded by the street railway industry. In 1935, for example, U.S. streetcar systems operated close to four times as many cars, and more than 20 times the track mileage, as did rapid transit lines in these four urban centers.

But if subway and elevated systems were few in number, or seemed overshadowed by the relative size of the streetcar systems, they had actually assumed an extraordinary importance in North American urban transit by the mid-1930's. In 1935 rapid transit systems in the four principal urban centers carried more than 2,250 million revenue passengers, a traffic which equalled more than 40 percent of the number carried by all American streetcar lines, and which represented almost 25 percent of total U.S. transit patronage.

And while other forms of electric traction have languished over the last half century, rapid transit has prospered. The original subway and elevated systems have been modernized and extended, and new systems have been built, By 1988 the number of North American urban areas operating rapid transit systems had grown to almost four times the level of the 1930's, and subway and elevated railway systems had grown to a total of well over 800 route-miles.

Development of America's "first generation" of rapid transit railways dated to the late 19th and early 20th centuries. The earliest efforts to develop rapid transit lines were in New York City, which had ranked as the nation's largest urban center since the early 1800's. By 1870, when New York's population was approaching a million, the city's streetcar and omnibus lines were transporting more than 115 million passengers annually, and the city was suffering from severe traffic congestion. There had been proposals for steam-powered subways on Manhattan as early as 1864, but none of them ever reached the construction stage. Inventor Alfred Ely Beach opened a short experimental pneumatic subway under Broadway in 1870, but plans to build a 5-mile Beach subway failed.

New York finally got its first regular rapid transit service in 1871, when the New York Elevated Railroad began operation between Battery Place and 30th Street. Designed by engineer Charles T. Harvey, the line was originally planned and built with a cable-propulsion system. This proved unsatisfactory and it was converted to steam power, with trains pulled by small steam dummy engines. A second Manhattan elevated company, the Metropolitan Elevated Railway, opened a line on Sixth Avenue in 1878. Consolidated into the Manhattan Railway, New York's elevated system grew rapidly; by 1880 the city's Els were carrying more than 60 million annual passengers. Elevated trains were running across the Brooklyn Bridge soon after it opened in 1883, and Brooklyn's first El commenced operation in 1885.

Chicago became the second North American city to enjoy rapid transit service when the South Side Elevated Railway opened in 1891. Over the next decade three more Chicago "L" companies began operation, and by 1900 the city had a comprehensive 91-mile system of elevated railways.

While the early lines in New York and Chicago employed steam power, electrification experiments were being conducted on the New York elevateds as early as 1885. Chicago's Metropolitan West Side line opened with electric power in 1895, and within less than a decade the Chicago and New York elevated railway systems had completed a conversion to electric power. The first Chicago "L" electrifications employed a locomotive-drawn train arrangement, with a single heavy motorized passenger car pulling a string of trailers. In 1897, however, electric traction pioneer Frank J. Sprague developed a multiple unit system of electric train control for electrification of Chicago's South Side Elevated, and this much superior arrangement quickly became the standard for rapid transit electrification.

While a steam-powered subway had opened in London, England, as early as 1863, it was not until the development of electrification that subways became a really practical form of urban rapid transit. The first North American subway had been the Tremont Street trolley subway in Boston, which opened in 1897. In 1901 this became the first American rapid transit subway as well, when trains of Boston's first rapid transit line, the Sullivan Square-Dudley Street subway-elevated line, began operating through the Tremont subway. Other subway and elevated lines were added to the Boston system over the next two decades, and by the early 1920's Boston had almost 40 miles of rapid transit railways.

New York city began construction of its first subway, the Interborough Rapid Transit, in 1900, and the line's first section was carrying more than 400,000 daily passengers within the first year after its opening in 1904. Subway construction continued almost without interruption thereafter, and by the late 1930's the city's subway and elevated system totaled well over 200 route-miles and was transporting over 4 million daily passengers in the boroughs of Manhattan, The Bronx, Queens, and Brooklyn.

Two other major rapid transit systems had been established in the New York metropolitan area in the early part of the century. A project to provide transit service beneath the Hudson River between New Jersey and Manhattan had finally been realized after more than 30 years of effort with completion of the Hudson Tubes and the opening of the Hudson & Manhattan Railway in 1908. By the time the H&M reached its full extent three years later, the system linked Newark and Hoboken with two Manhattan terminals. Rapid transit service had come to Richmond, New York City's fifth borough, in 1925 with the electrification of the Staten Island Rapid Transit Railway, a Baltimore & Ohio subsidiary.

Philadelphia had acquired its first rapid transit service in 1905, when the Market Street subway-elevated began operating between the Delaware River and the 69th Street terminal in Upper Darby. An elevated extension of the line opened to Frankford in 1920, and the first segment of the north-south Broad Street Subway began operating in 1928.

While street railways and interurbans were in a state of rapid decline, the late 1930's were a time of growth and expansion for America's several rapid transit systems. Between 1932 and 1937 more than 50 miles of subway had been added to the New York City system. At Philadelphia a new line across the great Delaware River suspension bridge linked downtown Philadelphia with Camden, N.J., in 1936. Two years later a major extension of the Broad Street subway opened to Snyder Avenue, south of downtown Philadelphia. At Chicago, where the elevated system had remained almost unchanged since the beginning of the century, the city began construction of its first subway, a 5-mile line under State Street, in 1938. Construction for a second Chicago subway, a 4-mile Milwaukee-Congress-Dearborn route, began a year later.

Through the 1930's and beyond, rolling stock for North America's rapid transit systems consisted almost entirely of what might be termed "first generation" wood or steel cars. Typically, these were double truck cars equipped with multiple unit control systems for train operation. Until the turn of the century, wooden construction was standard for elevated railway rolling stock. Many of these elevated cars were originally built as trailers for steam-powered trains, and were simply equipped with motor trucks and multiple unit control equipment when the lines were electrified.

For a time wooden cars operated on Boston's first elevated-subway rapid transit line, and New York's IRT opened in 1904 with a fleet of wood and steel "composite" cars. But even before the IRT opened, Pennsylvania Railroad engineer George Gibbs had designed a prototype car for the IRT that represented the world's first all-steel passenger car. A fleet of Gibbs cars was ordered for the IRT, and the use of all-steel equipment soon became the standard for subways in New York and other cities.

An early innovation in rapid transit car design had been the development in the 1920's of a three-section articulated car by New York's Brooklyn Manhattan Transit (BMT), which acquired 121 of these "triplex" units during 1927-28. The success of the triplex units led to the development of two experimental five-unit articulated trains for the BMT in 1934. Both of these 170-foot trains were equipped with advanced mechanical and electrical equipment, and employed lightweight car body construction to permit operation over sections of the New York elevated system that were unable to support the heavier standard steel subway cars. A "Green Hornet" prototype built by Pullman-Standard employed aluminum construction to obtain the necessary weight reduction, while the second prototype, built by the Budd Company, employed the builder's innovative shot-welded corrugated stainless steel construction. Two years after these "multi-section" prototypes went into operation, the BMT ordered 25 similar multi-section trains of lightweight low-alloy, high-tensile steel construction.

Still another BMT rolling stock experiment followed the development of the PCC streetcar. In 1938 the company ordered a three-unit articulated train from the Clark Equipment Company that incorporated lightweight aluminum construction, and standard PCC trucks and control equipment. In addition to its advanced technical features, the Clark "Bluebird" also provided a much higher standard of passenger comfort than New York rapid transit passengers were accustomed to seeing. The experiment was a success, and 50 more of the articulated trains were ordered in 1940. That same year, however, the three New York rapid transit operating companies were consolidated into a single city-owned system. A preference for more conventional heavyweight rolling stock prevailed within the new agency, and the PCC-type Bluebirds were to prove one of New York's last innovative ventures in rapid transit equipment for many years. Indeed, the BMT order was cancelled by the new city agency after only five of the advanced trains had been delivered.

An improving economy and continued urban growth both contributed to a modest increase in North American rapid transit ridership during the latter half of the 1930's. By 1940, on the eve of U.S. entry into World War II, annual subway and elevated railway traffic had grown to almost 2,282 million riders. Wartime travel demands led to still more growth; by 1945 rapid transit ridership had reached a peak of over 2,555 million annual passengers, an increase of more than 10 percent over the 1940 level.

There was both growth and retrenchment for North American rapid transit systems during the 1940's and 1950's. At Chicago, the new State Street subway begun in 1938 went into service in 1943. Construction of the Milwaukee-Dearborn-Congress subway was interrupted by the war, and the 4-mile line didn't open until 1951.

At New York there was mostly retrenchment. Consolidation of the IRT, BMT, and Independent systems in 1940 was accompanied by large scale abandonment of the old elevated systems. Portions of the BMT's Fulton Street El and the entire 5th Avenue elevated were closed, while the entire IRT 9th Avenue line and most of the 2nd Avenue El were abandoned. Of the city's four original elevated railways, only the 3rd Avenue El remained in full operation after the 1940 consolidation, and this line, too, was finally closed in 1955.

Although there was no major new construction, two new lines were added to the great New York City rapid transit system. A 4-mile section of the abandoned New York, Westchester & Boston was added to the city system in 1941, extending IRT service to Dyre Avenue in the Bronx. A major 11-mile extension of the New York system went into service in 1956, when Transit Authority trains began running across Jamaica Bay to the Rockaways over a newly rebuilt line that had been acquired from the Long Island Rail Road after fire destroyed the Jamaica Bay trestle in 1940.

Boston's rapid transit system opened one major new line in the immediate post-war period. Trains began running in 1952 over a 2-mile extension of the East Boston subway line to Orient Heights that had been laid down in the former right-of-way of the electrified Boston, Revere Beach & Lynn, which had been abandoned in 1940. A further 2-mile extension of the line to Revere Beach opened in 1954.

Through the mid-century point, North American rapid transit remained confined to the four major urban centers which had developed their systems in the late 19th and early 20th centuries. But finally, in the early 1950's, two important new systems were becoming realities.

The first of these to get underway was at Toronto, where subway proposals went back as far as 1910. By the late 1940's a plan had been adopted by the Toronto Transit Commission for a Yonge Street subway that would replace a streetcar route on which traffic had become so heavy that as many as 70 trolley-trailer trains were in rush hour operation. Construction began in 1949 and the

4.6-mile line opened between Union Station and Eglinton early in 1954. A second TTC subway, the 2-mile University line, opened in 1963, while the first 8-mile segment of the east-west Bloor-Danforth subway began operating in 1966. Extensions to both the Yonge and Bloor-Danforth lines were under construction almost continuously through 1980, and in 1978 TTC opened a 6-mile Spadina rapid transit line to the northwest that was linked to the University subway. By 1980 Toronto's rapid transit system encompassed over 35 route-miles, and was carrying well in excess of 800,000 daily passengers.

Cleveland became the next city to acquire a rapid transit system. Early in 1952 construction began on an east-west rapid transit line that had first been proposed more than 30 years before by the Van Sweringen brothers, the Cleveland real estate developers who had built both the Cleveland Union Terminal and the Shaker Heights Rapid Transit light rail line. The new Cleveland line was a relatively low cost route, located almost entirely on the surface within existing railroad rights-of-way. An initial section of the line opened between Cleveland Union Terminal and Windermere, some 8 miles to the east, in 1955. Two additional sections, completed in 1959 and 1968, extended rapid transit service 11 miles west to Cleveland's Hopkins Airport.

As these new rapid transit systems were being developed at Cleveland and Toronto during the latter part of the 1950's, there was a growing level of new construction and improvement on the original North American systems, too, as they grew to accommodate continuing urban and suburban growth.

The Chicago Transit Authority was clearly a leader among the original systems in expansion and improvement. The first of a series of major Chicago projects was also a prototype for what was to prove a popular form of multimodal urban transport, the combination of an urban expressway with a center median rapid transit line. This was the new high speed Congress rapid transit line, replacing the Garfield Park elevated, which was developed in the center median of the Eisenhower Expressway. The first segment of the the 10-mile line was opened during June 1958. The Skokie Swift, a high-speed service established on 5 miles of former North Shore Line track in Chicago's northern suburbs was an innovative addition to the CTA

system in April 1964. A second major expressway median line, a 9.5-mile north-south route in the Dan Ryan Expressway to 95th Street, went into service in September 1969. This was followed by several extensions to the northwest in the Kennedy Expressway median from the old Logan Square elevated terminal, first to Jefferson Park in February 1970 then to River Road in February 1983 and eventually reaching a new terminal at Chicago's O'Hare Airport in September 1984. Work began on still another major new Chicago route, a 9-mile southwestern line to Midway Airport, in 1986.

Boston's Massachusetts Bay Transportation Authority, too, carried out a number of major extension and improvement projects. The Cambridge-Dorchester-Ashmont "Red Line" rapid transit route was extended some 6 miles from South Boston to Quincy in 1971 over a route built in the right-of-way of the former Old Colony Line of the New Haven Railroad. A further 3-mile extension of this South Shore route opened to Braintree early in 1980, while a 3-mile northwest subway extension of the Red Line from Harvard Square to Alewife was completed in 1983. Except for the original Washington Street subway in downtown Boston, MBTA's Orange Line—the old "Main Line Elevated"—was entirely replaced with new construction over a 20-year period beginning in 1967. The 6-mile Haymarket North extension, completed in 1977, replaced the old elevated route via Sullivan Square to Everett. The project included a new subway under the Charles River, linked with the downtown subway, and a new rapid transit route to Oak Grove in a Boston & Maine right-of-way. The massive Southwest Corridor project, completed in 1987, combined an entirely new Orange Line route to Forest Hills with a grade-separated relocation of main line railroad tracks in the corridor.

At New York City, work began in the 1970's on two major extensions to the city's rapid transit system. Construction began late in 1969 for a double-deck East 63rd Street tunnel under the East River that would carry both subway and Long Island Rail Road trains into Manhattan from Queens. Three years later work began on the long-planned, 13-mile Second Avenue subway that would add badly needed additional rapid transit capacity on Manhattan's east side. New York's massive financial problems of the 1970's, however, delayed completion of both projects, and New Yorkers are still waiting for their new subways. Aside from these projects, New York's rapid transit improvements have largely been confined to badly needed rehabilitation and modernization of the existing system.

At Philadelphia, only a single rapid transit extension was completed. This was a mile-long southward extension of the Broad Street subway to Pattison Avenue.

After World War II, leadership in rapid transit equipment development largely passed from New York to Chicago. In 1949 the New York City system initiated one more trial of PCC rapid transit technology with an order for ten Budd-built stainless steel subway cars that incorporated a special PCC rapid transit truck design and other PCC features. The experiment was not particularly successful, and the New York system thereafter stayed resolutely with more conventional heavyweight car designs.

As early as the late 1930's, the Chicago Rapid Transit Company had begun planning for a PCC rapid transit car much like the BMT's 1938 "Bluebird" prototype at New York. CRT's Skokie shops completed a mock-up of a single unit car in 1939, but financial problems and World War II had prevented any further progress. At war's end in 1945, however, CRT ordered four experimental three-unit articulated trains that incorporated such features as PCC trucks, motors and control; magnetic track brakes; and a curved-side car body design that maintained the narrow floor level width necessary for Chicago "L" platform clearance, while permitting a wider car body above the floor level. Pullman-Standard and the St. Louis Car Company divided the prototype order. Following testing by the Chicago Transit Authority, which had succeeded the Chicago Rapid Transit in 1947, an order was placed with St. Louis Car for 130 PCC rapid transit cars in 1948. While retaining all of the PCC features of the prototypes, the production order reverted to a more conventional single unit design, with cars operated in two-car "married pairs," which permitted economies through the use of shared auxiliary equipment, and the elimination of two of the four operating cabs that would otherwise have been required. Another 70 similar cars were ordered in 1950.

CTA continued its "L" and subway equipment modernization through the 1950's with an innovative program under which the principal components of the city's PCC streetcar fleet were incorporated into new rapid transit cars. Confronted with a pressing need for completing the replacement of its huge fleet of obsolete wooden "L" cars, CTA came up with the idea of converting its streetcar fleet for rapid transit service. An initial experiment at simply modifying the streetcar carbodies into rapid transit cars proved infeasible, and the transformation was ultimately accomplished by building new rapid transit body shells, which were then outfitted with trucks, motors, control equipment, motor-generators, track brakes, seats, and other components from scrapped PCC streetcars. Ultimately, 570 new cars were completed in this manner over the period from 1954 to 1960.

Boston adopted the PCC technology, too, when 40 new cars were ordered from St. Louis Car in 1950 for the Metropolitan Transit Authority's East Boston extension to Revere Beach. These were relatively small cars that incorporated standard PCC streetcar components much like Chicago's new rapid transit fleet. Almost 200 additional PCC rapid transit cars were ordered from Pullman-Standard for the Boston system over the next decade. All of these were "high performance" cars much larger than the original East Boston order. Employing components developed experimentally at Chicago, they were fitted with 100 h.p. motors instead of the usual 55 h.p. PCC motors, and were capable of much higher acceleration rates and maximum speeds than previous PCC rapid transit equipment.

New York's Hudson & Manhattan Railroad became another high performance PCC car operator in 1958-59, when 50 new cars were delivered from St. Louis Car for operation through the Hudson Tubes between New Jersey and Manhattan. The cars were also noteworthy as the first air-conditioned rapid transit equipment.

Cleveland became still another user of PCC rapid transit equipment when the Cleveland Transit System's new east-west rapid transit line opened in 1955. St. Louis Car built a car for the CTS system that, except for the truck design, closely paralleled the cars built just a few years previous for the MTA's East Boston extension. A total of 68 cars were on hand for opening of the initial CTS section in 1955, while another 30 were delivered before the first section of the line's western extension was completed in 1959.

For subsequent equipment orders, however, Cleveland gave up the use of PCC type equipment. Based upon the new Toronto system's successful adoption of extremely large cars, CTS incorporated a 70-foot car body into the design of 30 stainless steel "Airporter" cars delivered by Pullman-Standard in 1967 and 1970 for the line's extension to the Hopkins Airport. Compared even to the lightweight PCC equipment, CTS was able to gain a weight reduction of nearly 25 percent through the use of a large car and lightweight materials. Similar large car standards were retained for a fleet of 60 74-foot, stainless steel cars delivered by Japan's Tokyo Car Corporation in 1985 to replace the line's original equipment.

Initially, Toronto's new Yonge Street subway was expected to employ lightweight PCC rapid transit equipment as well, but the TTC equipment acquisition took a much different direction. Cost proposals for PCC equipment received early in 1951 were considered excessive, and the Commission instead ordered a much larger and heavier conventional car from Great Britain's Gloucester Railway Carriage and Wagon Company. Gloucester initially supplied 106 cars during 1953-54, while an additional 34 cars were delivered during 1958-59 to provide additional capacity to meet traffic growth.

The first 100 cars delivered under the Gloucester order were of steel construction, and weighed nearly 43 tons. In an effort to reduce weight, the balance of the 106-car order was completed with all-aluminum car body construction, an experiment that was to provide a clear direction for all future TTC rapid transit rolling stock design. The use of aluminum reduced the weight of the Gloucester cars by fully six tons each, as well as provided a virtually maintenance-free exterior. For the 34 additional cars acquired from Gloucester a few years later TTC specified aluminum roof construction, which helped to reduce weight by about 4 tons per car.

Beginning with an order for 36 new cars delivered by the Montreal Locomotive Works during 1962-63 for the University subway, TTC specified an even larger car of all-aluminum construction that represented a remarkable achievement in weight reduction. Although these 74 foot 6 inch cars were almost 18 feet longer than the original Gloucester cars, they weighed less than 30 tons, almost 13 tons less than TTC's first rapid transit cars. They also represented the longest rapid transit cars in the world, with the lowest weight per linear or square foot yet attained.

These new M-1 cars represented impressive gains for TTC in performance characteristics, as well as in weight, maintenance cost, and power consumption reduction, and the basic design became a standard for future TTC orders. Through 1979 orders for an additional 462 similar cars for the expanding Toronto rapid transit system went to Hawker Siddeley Canada, while 126 more were supplied by UTDC/Can Car Rail during 1987-88 to replace the original Gloucester-built fleet.

Elsewhere, too, there was an increasing diversity in rolling stock design as the original North American systems continued to place sizable orders for the equipment needed both to replace their original fleets and for system expansion. Chicago's last PCC type rapid transit cars were delivered in 1959, and 96 Pullman-Standard cars delivered in 1963 for Boston's Red Line proved to be the last PCC type rapid transit equipment, although many later cars incorporated design features originated with the PCC.

At Chicago, four high-performance test cars delivered in 1960 had been equipped with 100 h.p. motors and experimental trucks, controls, and a variety of other components. This test program led to the development of specifications for a new generation of CTA high performance rapid transit cars. The first 180 of these new cars were delivered by Pullman-Standard during 1964, and incorporated such features as aluminum car bodies, molded fiberglass ends, air conditioning, a new truck design, and many other advanced components. A fleet of 150 cars built for CTA by Budd in 1969 were similar in design, except for their use of stainless steel car body construction and Budd's Pioneer III truck. A third major order for 200 comparable high performance cars, delivered by Boeing-Vertol during 1976-77 also employed stainless steel car bodies, and ten of the cars were equipped with advanced solid state chopper control and a regenerative braking capability. However, only two of these ten cars ran in Chicago. A third car went to General Electric at Erie, Pennsylvania for testing. In short order all ten cars were reequipped with standard equipment. Under the most recent CTA order, which went to Budd, a fleet of 600 similar cars delivered during 1981-87 provided the system with sufficient new rolling stock to substantially replace the original PCC type cars of the 1950's.

The New Jersey-New York Port Authority Trans-Hudson Corporation, which had replaced the old Hudson & Manhattan, followed Chicago's lead in 1965, when a new fleet of 162 modern rapid transit cars was delivered from St. Louis Car. Equally advanced as the CTA's new Pullman-Standard cars, the PATH equipment included such features as stainless steel construction, air conditioning, and high performance components that permitted maximum speeds of 70 m.p.h. Another 90 similar cars were supplied by St. Louis and Canada's Hawker Siddeley in 1967 and 1972, while another 95 cars were built by Japan's Kawasaki Heavy Industries during 1987 to help accommodate a steadily-growing PATH traffic that had reached more than 200,000 daily passengers.

Boston's MBTA adopted performance and comfort standards very similar to those developed by CTA and PATH for a 76-car fleet built by Pullman-Standard in 1969 to outfit the new South Shore extension of the Red Line. The 70-foot cars incorporated such features as aluminum body construction, air conditioning, and high performance motors, trucks and controls that permitted a 70 m.p.h. maximum speed. Similar standards were maintained by MBTA for 154 new cars received from Canada's Hawker Siddeley during 1980-81 as replacement equipment for the Orange and Blue Lines. Still another 58 modern cars for the Red Line were on order from Canada's UTDC for 1988 delivery.

Philadelphia acquired its first modern rapid transit equipment in 1960, when the Budd Company delivered a new fleet of 270 stainless steel cars to replace original equipment on the Market-Frankford subway-elevated route. The Broad Street subway continued to operate with its original 1920's equipment until 1982, when Japan's Kawasaki began delivery of a replacement fleet of 125 modern stainless steel cars.

The extraordinary New York subway system, which transports a weekday traffic of some 3.6 million passengers, represented a rolling stock market that dwarfed all other North American rapid transit systems combined. The system had continued to operate largely with its original rolling stock through the end of World War II, and replacement of this enormous fleet over the four decades

after the war required the delivery of some 8,000 subway cars from every major U.S. builder and, more recently, suppliers in Canada, France, and Japan.

Aside from the several trials with experimental equipment already noted, a highly conservative approach to rolling stock design prevailed on the New York system, and advances in rapid transit equipment technology were largely left to other systems. The basic pattern for New York subway car design through much of the post-war period had been set as far back as 1930, when the R-1 car was designed for the city's Independent subway. The R-1 was a 60-foot, heavyweight steel car of determinedly utilitarian design, and it was a sturdy, serviceable car that held up well in the punishing New York service.

Descendants of the R-1 continued to roll off the car builders' assembly lines for the New York system through the end of the 1960's. A 300-car order that went to Budd in 1965 was turned out with stainless steel car bodies that achieved appreciable weight reductions, but the cars were otherwise comparable to the standard New York unit. Two orders delivered by St. Louis in the late 1960's included some air conditioned cars, and the second of the two orders—the R-40 car—represented New York's first attempt to develop a stylized car. A 400-car R-42 fleet delivered by St. Louis during 1968-69 featured molded fiberglass ends, stainless steel exteriors, and air conditioning. Even so, however, the R-42 was not a full break from the R-1 tradition, for even these handsome new cars retained the basic dimensions set by the 1930 cars, and they were operationally compatible with earlier New York equipment.

Finally, New York broke with previous practice with a 300-car R-44 order delivered by St. Louis Car during 1970-71. The R-44 was a 75-foot car, the longest ever built for the New York subways, and it was capable of speeds up to 80 m.p.h., even though the cars would be limited to 50 m.p.h. until the Second Avenue subway became available. Exterior appearance of the new cars was similar to the previous R-42 cars. Another 52 R-44 cars were delivered for service on the Staten Island Rapid Transit which, together with the New York Transit Authority, had become part of the New York region Metropolitan Transportation Authority in 1969. Pullman-Standard supplied 754 R-46 cars during 1974-78 that were nearly identical to the R-44's, except for New York's first application of an air suspension system. Another 225 similar R-68 cars, together with 1,150 smaller R-62 cars for IRT lines, were being supplied during the mid-1980's under a massive 5-year Transit Authority improvement program.

New York subway car design promised to become even more innovative in the 1990's. Late in 1987 the Transit Authority was seeking suppliers to develop prototype A.C. traction motor cars. Orders could eventually reach 1,500 cars, with an initial order for 200 to be placed in 1992.

Both the original rapid transit systems at New York, Boston, Philadelphia and Chicago, and the newer systems at Toronto and Cleveland, represented what might be called a "first generation" of rapid transit technology. As an expanding American population and urban growth generated an increasing demand for improved transit services during the 1960's, a new rapid transit technology began to emerge. This new technology took advantage of modern advances in computerization and electronics to develop highly sophisticated and automated systems for train operation and control, fare collection, and the like. Advances in materials technology, and in control and propulsion systems, were applied to the development of radically different rolling stock. Perhaps most important of all in an era when public transit was competing as never before with the private automobile as an alternative, this new generation of transit systems reflected an extraordinary emphasis on the development of facilities and equipment that were appealing, comfortable, and convenient.

Supporting this development of new rapid transit systems was the growing level of public support to transit during the 1950's and 1960's. The shift from private ownership to public agency operation typically brought new funding support from tax revenues for capital and operating expenses. Beginning with the Urban Mass Transportation Act of 1964, major federal funding became available for capital grants to transit projects. A decade later this was followed by a broadening of the federal program to include operating funds.

The first of these "new generation" rapid transit systems to become a reality was in New Jersey, where construction began in 1964 on an extension of the Port Authority Transit Corporation's Philadelphia-Camden line that would create an entirely new 14-mile high-speed line between Philadelphia and suburban Lindenwold. Following what was to become a frequent practice with new rapid transit systems, the new PATCO line was laid largely in existing railroad right-of-way, in this case the Pennsylvania-Reading Seashore Lines. The line's link to downtown Philadelphia, a section of downtown subway and the Benjamin Franklin Bridge line that had opened in 1936, was thoroughly upgraded to the technical standards of the new line.

Operation of the Lindenwold line was automated to an unprecedented level. Trains operated under the control of an Automatic Train Operation (ATO) system. Fare collection was fully automated through the use of ticket vending machines that dispensed magnetically encoded tickets, and automatic fare gates. Security was provided to the line's 14 unmanned stations through the use of remotely monitored closed circuit television. Park-and-ride lots at PATCO's suburban stations provided convenient access to the high-speed trains for automobile commuters.

A fleet of 76 large, stainless steel cars was built by Budd for the new line. Trucks were the Budd Pioneer III type with an air suspension system, while four 160 h.p. motors gave the cars a 75 m.p.h. maximum operating speed capability.

Opening early in 1969, the Lindenwold line proved an immediate success. Within only a few years, the Lindenwold trains were transporting more than 10 million passengers annually, and the line's automation features had permitted PATCO to attain one of the highest revenue-to-expense operating ratios in the U.S. transit industry.

While the Lindenwold project was moving rather quietly and uneventfully from construction to operation, another, and much more ambitious, project on the West Coast was getting all of the attention. This was a regional high speed rapid transit system being developed for the San Francisco Bay Area by the Bay Area Rapid Transit District. BART had become a reality when Bay Area voters had approved a $792 million bond issue in 1962 that was to finance the 71-mile, three-county system.

Recognizing that the new Bay Area system had to compete with the automobile far more effectively than any of the traditional transit systems in eastern urban centers, BART's engineers adopted extraordinarily high design standards intended to establish a wholly new level of performance, passenger comfort, and aesthetic appeal that could attract the freeway commuter away from his automobile.

Linking San Francisco with the East Bay, the BART system comprised a single San Francisco route between Daly City and the downtown area that was joined to the East Bay by a new tube under San Francisco Bay. At Oakland, routes branched north, east, and south to Richmond, Concord, and Fremont. Altogether, BART required the construction of some 25 double-track route miles at grade level, another 25 miles of elevated structure, and 23 miles of underground construction, including the 3.6-mile tube under San Francisco Bay and a 3.1-mile hard rock tunnel through the Berkeley Hills.

Standards for the BART fixed plant reflected BART's ambitious goals. Track alignment and construction standards were adequate to permit a planned 80 m.p.h. maximum operating speed. A 5-foot 6-inch track gauge was adopted to provide stability at high speeds for the extremely lightweight trains. Track was laid with continuously welded rail, supported by prestressed concrete ties on at-grade sections, and directly fastened to concrete supporting slabs on elevated or subway track. The system incorporated a total of 34 handsome stations, with extensive park-and-ride lots at all of the system's suburban stations. Elevated sections of the line were constructed with precast, prestressed concrete girders, and landscaped "linear parks" were established beneath the structures to create an atmosphere quite different from the original eastern elevated railways.

Computers and electronics technology were employed to outfit BART with such features as an Automatic Train Control system that permitted train operation in a fully automatic mode. Central computers in the BART headquarters at Lake Merritt governed operation of the entire system. Mini computers at each station operated train destination signs that were activated by coded signals from approaching trains. Ticket vending and fare collection were fully automated, utilizing a magnetically coded fare card that had a "stored fare" capability.

Perhaps the most radical advances of all made by BART were

in the design standards for the 80 m.p.h. BART car. Configuration, interior arrangement, passenger amenities, and appearance of the car were developed by the Detroit industrial design firm of Sundberg-Ferar, while details of its design and construction were developed by the car builder. Instead of going to one of the traditional car builders, the BART production order went to the Rohr Corporation, a San Diego aerospace manufacturer, which applied a variety of aerospace materials and methods to the production of an eventual total of 450 BART cars that were delivered during 1970-75.

Configuration of the cars represented a departure from conventional rapid transit practice, with trains made up from two basic car types. A 75-foot "A" control car at each end was fitted with a molded fiberglass streamlined cab, while the remainder of each train of up to ten cars was made up of 70-foot mid-train "B" cars. The Rohr aerospace design utilized monocoque construction, in which the entire car body is an integral, load carrying structure. Sidewalls, fabricated as a single aluminum extrusion, were riveted together with roof panels, floor beams, and floor panels to complete an integrated body structure. The roof panel was fabricated of aluminum alloy sandwiched with foam, while an inner lining of molded fiberglass was riveted to the roof structure. Floor panels were a metal sandwich structure, with an outer skin of aluminum bonded to a foam core.

The innovative Rohr design produced what was the lightest high-speed transit car ever produced, with an average weight of only about 800 pounds per seat.

An LFM-Rockwell truck developed for BART employed an articulated cast steel frame with inside bearings. An air bag suspension system was fitted with leveling valves controlled by a load weighing system. Four 150 h.p. motors provided sufficient power for a 3 m.p.h. per second acceleration rate and the car's designed 80 m.p.h. top speed. Control was provided by a solid-state thyristor "chopper" system.

Interiors of the cars incorporated such passenger comfort features as foam padded seating upholstered in fabric and vinyl, carpeting, and, of course, air conditioning.

BART's first construction, a 4.4-mile test track at Mt. Diablo, began in 1964, but it was not until 1972 that the first BART trains began carrying passengers, and the full system was not in operation until 1974, when the Transbay Tube opened to regular service.

Beset with almost endless problems, BART represented a major Bay Area controversy throughout its early years. Inflation drove construction costs far above the original budget; when the system was finally completed, its cost of $1.6 billion was nearly double the original budget. BART trains didn't make it from the East Bay to San Francisco until 1974, four years behind schedule. And when the system finally did begin running it was plagued with train control system problems that precluded the full planned level of operation for several years until they were finally corrected. Myriad faults with the sophisticated car gave BART major equipment reliability problems; at times little more than half of the car fleet was operable, and five or six trains were failing daily out of a total of 22 trains in service.

But gradually the problems were solved, and BART became the reliable, high-speed rapid transit system it was intended to be. BART ridership climbed steadily to reach a daily average of more than 200,000, and the availability of BART service contributed to major economic growth in downtown San Francisco. By the mid-1980's major expansion of the BART system was close at hand. Deliveries of an additional 150 cars from France's Alsthom-Atlantique began in 1987, work was underway at Daly City on new facilities that will give the system a substantially increased rush hour capacity and its first station in San Mateo County, and planning was moving ahead on BART extensions eastward into Contra Costa and Alameda counties, and southward to the San Francisco Airport and into Santa Clara County.

The new age of rapid transit technology initiated by Lindenwold and BART soon encouraged new projects in other American urban centers.

At Washington, D.C., the Washington Metropolitan Area Transportation Authority began construction in 1969 on a high-speed system that employed design standards comparable to those adopted by BART. The regional system was planned to link the District of Columbia with suburban terminals in Maryland and Virginia. An initial 4.5-mile WMATA segment opened between Rhode Island Avenue and downtown Washington in 1976, and the system grew steadily thereafter. By the time Metro's Orange Line reached its planned terminal at Vienna, Virginia, in 1986, the system had grown to a total of almost 70 miles, with 64 stations, and Metro trains were carrying well over 400,000 daily passengers. Completion of the full 103-mile, $9.4 billion system is currently forecast for 1997.

Aerospace manufacturer Rohr supplied WMATA with an initial fleet of 300 75-foot, aluminum bodied cars during 1975-76 that owed much in their construction details and design features to the BART car. After suffering severe losses on the Washington order, Rohr quit the rail car field, and WMATA's next order, for 294 similar cars, went to Italy's Breda Costruzioni Ferroviarie in the early 1980's.

Atlanta, Georgia, became the next urban center to join the new rapid transit boom, when the Metropolitan Atlanta Rapid Transit Authority began construction in 1975 of a planned 53-mile, 39-station regional system that incorporated a rapid transit technology comparable to both the BART and WMATA systems. The planned system consisted of north-south and east-west trunk lines, intersecting at Five Points in downtown Atlanta, and several branches. Substantial portions of the east-west route opened in 1979, while the first north-south segment began running three years later. By 1986, when the north-south route had reached a total length of 15 miles, MARTA traffic had reached 65 million annual passengers. The last section of the southern end of the north-south line was scheduled to open into Atlanta's Hartsfield International Airport by late 1988, with the full 53-mile system expected to be completed by 2000.

MARTA's rolling stock design incorporated the same sort of large, lightweight car body; passenger comfort and aesthetic features; and high performance characteristics that BART and WMATA had pioneered for the new generation of rapid transit systems. The 75-foot, aluminum cars weighed only 38 tons each. Four 172 h.p. traction motors permitted a 3 m.p.h. per second acceleration rate and a 70 m.p.h. top speed. France's Franco Belge supplied an initial 120 cars during 1978-82, while a further 100 cars were delivered by Japan's Hitachi during 1983-87.

Baltimore and Miami were the next cities to develop new

generation rapid transit systems, both of which were built to similar design characteristics. The Maryland Mass Transit Administration began construction of an initial segment of the Baltimore system, extending 8 miles northwest to a Reisterstown Plaza terminal, in 1976. The combined subway and elevated route opened in 1983, while a further 6-mile, at-grade extension to Owings Mills went into service four years later. By the time the full route was in service, Baltimore Metro traffic had reached a daily level of 45,000 passengers, and planning was underway for a 2-mile eastern extension that would link the system's downtown terminal with the Johns Hopkins Hospital area.

At Miami, the Metro Dade Transportation Administration began work in 1979 on a 21-mile elevated rapid transit route that linked downtown Miami with Dadeland South to the southwest and Okeechobee to the northwest. At its downtown Government Center station, Metrorail was linked to a 2-mile Metromover "people mover" system which acted as a downtown distributor for the rail system. The full 21-mile route opened in two stages during 1984, while the Metromover system began running in 1986. One of the few new systems to fall far short of its passenger traffic projections, Miami's Metrorail was transporting barely 35,000 passengers in 1987, against pre-opening predictions of as many as 200,000 daily riders. Although this disappointing start had placed the future of planned extensions to a 50-mile system by 2000 in doubt, the city was moving ahead with extensions of nearly 2 miles to the downtown Metromover connection.

Rolling stock requirements for the Baltimore and Miami systems were combined into a single order that went to the Budd Company for 208 75-foot stainlesss steel high speed cars that virtually duplicated the performance characteristics of the earlier Washington and Atlanta fleets. Baltimore received 72 of the Budd cars during 1982-84, while 136 were delivered to Miami during the same period. Another 28 cars were delivered to the Baltimore Metro under a contract option in time for the opening of the Owings Mills extension.

While U.S. rapid transit development stayed with the time-honored steel-wheel-on-steel-rail-concept, two other new North America systems adopted a novel new rubber-tired transit technol-ogy originated in France.

Reflecting a Quebecois orientation to French culture and technology, Montreal adopted the rubber-tired system developed by the Paris Metro for a new Montreal Metro project which began in 1962. The French system employed rubber-tired trucks operating on 10-inch-wide reinforced concrete "running rails," with smaller horizontal tires bearing against steel guide rails acting as lateral guide wheels. Flanged steel safety wheels and steel safety rails provided guidance at switches and in case of tire failure. Advantages claimed for the rubber-mounted system were noise and vibration reduction, and improved traction, which permitted operation on steeper gradients. The entire system was to be in subway, much of it drilled through solid rock.

Reflecting both the more urban nature of the Montreal system, and the weight limitations of the rubber-tired format, Metro rolling stock was somewhat more modest in both size and performance characteristics than the large, high-speed cars that were to become typical of the new generation of high-speed regional systems in North American cities over the next two decades. Each Metro motor car was only 55 feet long and 8 feet 3 inches wide, and weighed 30 tons. Cars were operated in three-car sets of two motor and one trailer car, with a maximum train length of three sets. Four 155 h.p. traction motors on each power car developed a maximum acceleration rate of 3 m.p.h. per second and a 50 m.p.h. top speed. The maximum operating speed for the system was limited by the relatively close station spacing. The average distance between stations was 2300 feet, with some less than 1500 feet apart.

An initial Metro fleet of 369 cars was supplied by Canadian-Vickers during 1965-66, while a subsequent 423 nearly identical cars were built for the growing system by Quebec's Bombardier during the mid-1970's.

The first sections of the Montreal Metro opened in 1966, and by the following spring a system of three lines totaling over 16 miles was in service. Metro ridership in its first full year, when the trains helped to carry record traffic to Montreal's Expo 67, reached more than 136 million. Steady expansion of the system has continued ever since. By 1987 the Société de transport de la Communaute de Montréal (STCUM) was operating a four-line, 62-station Metro of some 33 miles, with a further 7 miles of subway under construction. By 1985, ridership on the Metro had reached some 206 million annual passengers.

The same French rubber-tired technology was applied to a new rapid transit system for Mexico City, which began to take shape in 1967. Aided by both French loans and a French technical consortium, as many as 10,000 Mexican construction workers toiled on around-the-clock schedules to complete the city's first 9.4-mile Metro route in only 27 months. A full three-line, 26-mile system, most of in it subway, was in operation by the end of 1970. Soon after the full system opened, Mexico City's subway was transporting close to two million daily passengers. Construction of a second stage of Metro extensions and new lines totaling almost 28 miles began in 1977, and a 16-mile third stage began in 1981. By 1987 the city's Sistema de Transporte Collectivo (STC) was operating a system of eight lines, 116 stations, and 82 miles of line, some 48 miles of it in subway. Traffic on the intensively utilized system was more than 1.3 billion passengers each year, with a record one-day peak of 4.3 million riders. Another 18 miles of Metro was under construction toward a year 2010 master plan goal of a 20-line, 274-mile Metro network for Mexico's capitol city.

Rolling stock for the Mexico City Metro was comparable in both size and performance characteristics to that built for the Montreal system, with cars operated in three-car motor-trailer-motor sets, with trains made up of up to three sets. An initial 537-car order was delivered by France's CIMT and Brissoneau et Lotz in 1969. Additional cars supplied from Alsthom raised the total number of French-built cars on the system to more than 1000 by 1983. Canada's Bombardier, which had previously supplied over 400 similar rubber-tired cars to the Montreal Metro, landed a 180-car order from Mexico City in 1981. At the same time Mexico's own Constructora Nacional de Carros de Ferrocarril (CNCF) began to supply equipment for STC's steadily growing Metro network. By 1987 the system's rolling stock fleet had reached a total of well over 2000 cars.

Some two decades after work began on the Montreal Metro, Canada once again became a North American innovator in rapid transit technology. Developed beginning in the mid-1970's by

Canada's Urban Transportation Development Corporation (UTDC), this new technology, designed to provide both a passenger capacity and capital cost range midway between those of conventional light rail and heavy rapid transit, was called Intermediate Capacity Transit System, or ICTS. Incorporating a broad range of technical innovations, ICTS clearly represented the most comprehensive application of new transit technology in a single system since the start of the BART project.

In the linear induction motor, or LIM, propulsion system developed for ICTS, half of the traction motor, in effect, was placed in the track. A linear motor, corresponding to the flattened stator of a conventional rotary motor, was suspended under each truck with a nominal clearance of only about a half-inch above a 12-inch wide continuous steel reaction rail placed between the running rails. This reaction rail corresponded to the rotor of a conventional motor, flattened and laid continuously in the track. The LIM was powered by variable voltage and frequency three-phase A.C. supplied from a solid state chopper-inverter in each car.

Other features of ICTS included regenerative braking, a steerable axle truck design that promised reductions in both noise levels and rail-wheel wear, and a fully automatic, close headway control system that permitted a 40 second minimum headway. Through the use of fiberglass, welded aluminum, a honeycomb aluminum roof and a honeycomb plymetal floor, UTDC was able to develop a lightweight carbody that kept total car weight to less than 15 tons for the standard 42-foot-long, 8-foot-wide ICTS car. Maximum operating speed for ICTS was 50 m.p.h., with a 2.24 m.p.h. per second acceleration rate.

Development of the ICTS technology was begun by UTDC in 1975, and reached the state of prototype test operation by 1978. ICTS got its first commercial application at Toronto after the Toronto Transit Commission decided to convert its planned Scarborough light rail line to the new technology. Linking the eastern terminal of TTC's Bloor-Danforth subway with the Scarborough Town Centre, the 4.3-mile line opened to service in the spring of 1985 with a fleet of 24 ICTS cars operating in two-car married pairs. Although the system was capable of fully automatic operation, TTC elected to provide an operator on each train.

A much more ambitious ICTS installation at Vancouver, B.C., followed closely behind the TTC application. Vancouver had originally planned a regional light rail system, but B.C. Transit decided in 1980 to shift to the ICTS technology in order to assure adequate potential for future capacity growth. Construction of a 13.3-mile Vancouver-New Westminster route was initiated on a "fast track" basis in order to have the line in operation in time for Vancouver's Expo '86. The selected route included both at-grade and elevated track, largely in the right-of-way of the abandoned British Columbia Electric Railway's New Westminster interurban route, and reached its downtown Vancouver terminal through a 1.2-mile subway installed in an abandoned Canadian Pacific tunnel. A fleet of 114 standard ICTS vehicles was supplied by UTDC's Venture Trans subsidiary at Kingston, Ontario.

Skytrain, as B.C. Transit called the new system, went into operation right on schedule late in 1985. Although on-board train attendants were on duty, the system operated on a fully automatic basis. Remarkably free of the sort of problems that so often accompany new technologies, Skytrain was an early success, transporting a daily traffic of as many as 170,000 passengers during Expo '86. By late spring of 1986 construction was underway on a three-mile extension across the Fraser River to Surrey, with still other additions to the system planned.

A third application of ICTS technology opened for revenue service in mid-1987 at Detroit, where it had been adopted for a downtown people mover system. A fleet of 13 ICTS vehicles operated in a counter-clockwise direction around a 2.9-mile elevated loop.

With well over a dozen new or rehabilitated systems already operating, the resurgence of rail rapid transit in North America became complete one day late in September 1986 when Los Angeles, the largest city on the continent without any form of rail transit, broke ground for the first section of its planned Metro Rail subway. The event marked the culmination of more than three decades of planning, during which political controversies over routes for a regional rail system, failed efforts to establish a local funding base, and then disappearing federal financial support, had frustrated efforts to build a rail transit alternative to congested freeways in the third largest North American urban center. The project started in 1986 will provide a 4.4-mile route in the city's Wilshire Corridor that should be open by 1992. Eventually, the Southern California Rapid Transit District plans to extend the initial line to the San Fernando Valley, Santa Monica, and Downey to form the major trunk links of a comprehensive Los Angeles County regional system of light rail and rapid transit routes expected to reach an eventual total of 150 miles. Los Angeles, once the center of the greatest urban and interurban electric railway system in North America, had played out its love affair with the automobile, and electric traction was coming back.

Rapid transit in Chicago has always had special meaning to CERA. In part, it is because one of our founding members, George Krambles, spent 43 years at the Chicago Rapid Transit and later the Chicago Transit Authority, starting his career as a staff engineer in 1937 and retiring in 1980. Many people from places other than Chicago describe riding this system as fun. It is fun because there are very few subway miles and there is a variety of operations. ABOVE: For years, the personification of the Rapid Transit was the 4000's. The 455 cars in the series were built in two basic lots—the "baldies" (no trolley poles on their roofs) in 1914 and 1915, cars 4001-4250, and the "plushies" (plush seats) between 1922 and 1924, cars 4251-4455. In their prime, a train of "baldies" heads into the Loop on July 17, 1940. This view is looking northwest at the eastern most curve at North Avenue and Halsted Street. (GK Collection) FACING PAGE: The new era was introduced by the four 5000-series cars. 5001 and 5002 were built by Pullman, where the 5002 was photographed on August 14, 1947. 5003-5004 were built by St. Louis Car Co. These four cars introduced PCC technology to rapid transit operation. They were all electric cars which started the era of quick acceleration and deceleration of trains, characteristics for which Chicago's rapid transit operations are known. (GK Collection)

During the 50 years of CERA's existence, Chicago's rapid transit system went through many changes. Under the privately owned Chicago Rapid Transit Company (CRT), trains of orange and brown cars of a variety of two-motor cars pulling trailers plodded along. The combination of this equipment with many closely spaced stations made for a slow service. There were some rush hour expresses, but this usually meant gaps in the service to create track space, except on the North Side, where some four-track right-of-way existed. The successor public authority, Chicago Transit Authority (CTA), initiated a steady stream of changes. TOP LEFT: A single wooden car passed the east gate of the Chicago Union Stock Yards, circa 1950. The packing companies were already abandoning their Chicago plants, and service on the Stock Yards branch ended in 1957. The last wooden cars operated on CTA on December 1, 1957. TOP RIGHT: On July 16, 1939, car 4299 led two wooden cars on a southbound Jackson Park Express at Howard Street. Following the 1922-1924 delivery of cars 4251-4455, no new cars were received until the four 5000-series cars arrived in 1947 and 1948. Service lives of 50 years were typical for rapid transit cars in Chicago. BOTTOM: Two of the distinctive motor cars CRT inherited with its acquisition of the Metropolitan West Side Elevated Railroad Company were on either side of a trailer eastbound over what was then the Chicago Burlington & Quincy Railroad at the Douglas Park station on October 13, 1938. The cars in this train, from the rear, are 2844-2280 and 2814, which were built by ACF in 1904, 1900 and 1904, respectively. *(Three photos GK)* THIS PAGE TOP: In 1938 construction began on Chicago's first subways. On October 16, 1943, the inaugural train was southbound at Washington station, opening the State Street subway. Revenue service commenced the following day. BOTTOM: While construction of the Dearborn Street subway began at the same time as that on State Street, work was suspended due to shortages of critical materials needed for World War II, and the "biscuit-cutter" construction shield sat out the war years, headed south in the curve from Dearborn to Congress streets. On August 13, 1950, the first assignment of the new 6000-series cars was the Logan Square line. On January 23, 1951, a train of these cars was brought down to the Grand Avenue subway station and posed for pictures. Revenue service in the Dearborn Street subway began on February 25. On Saturday, February 24, 1951, between noon and 4:00 p.m., an open house was held for the new subway. Two eight-car empty 6000-class trains were brought in and split so that a single train, two-car unit was placed on the northbound track at each of the eight new subway stations for public inspection. After the open house, a six-car train was brought in and operated on the southbound track to demonstrate operating details for West Side supervisors. After everyone was satisfied, to close the day, the units were one by one accumulated into a single train of eight cars leaving LaSalle, ten at Jackson and so on. Leaving Lake Street Transfer, George Krambles took over to operate a 16-car train under the river crossing and on to the Evergreen portal, by which time it had 22 cars. This was a test to determine the limit of reliable MU train length. There was no trouble with propulsion circuits or with substations by holding to the P1 (low) accelerating rate. However, door control became erratic at a 16-car train length. *(Two photos Krambles Collection)*

In 1988, many railway museums have ex-Chicago 4000-series cars in their collections. For nearly six decades, this type of car was the pride of the fleet. From 1914 to 1943, these cars served throughout the system. From the opening of Chicago's first subway in 1943, all 455 of them were needed on that route until 1952, when 6000's began to take over and 4000's again appeared on other parts of the system. TOP LEFT: The first 250 steel cars had iron roofs uncluttered by equipment and ultimately acquired the nickname "baldies." A train of them was recorded on a Ravenswood run at Dearborn and Lake Streets on June 20, 1958, two days before the last streetcar run in Chicago and the opening of the Congress rapid transit line. TOP RIGHT: The later 205 steel cars had canvas-covered wooden roofs which carried trolley poles and many ventilators, but they acquired a nickname from their handsome green frieze plush seats as compared to the

rattan seats of the previous lot. This train of "plushies" was on the Lake line at Ridgeland and South Boulevard in Oak Park just prior to the 1962 relocation to the grade-separated line on the adjacent embankment that the Chicago & North Western Railway had built a half century before. BOTTOM: On November 8, 1973, car 4293 led the last trip of the 4000's in revenue service. The sign on the letter board says, "Good bye, old friends! I'm retiring today after 50 years." THIS PAGE: At 0900 hours on January 21, 1969, this was the view north from the Merchandise Mart over Franklin Street. Until October, 1943, the only access to the central business district from the North Side was over this double track elevated railway, threading its way through a loft manufacturing area symbolized by the hundreds of standpipe water tanks on roofs. The bunching of trains shown here was due to a delay of about 15 minutes, but, until the subway became available as an alternate route, as many as 73 trains passed here on each track during the peak hour and a scene like this would indicate a quiet minute. Automatic train control with cab signals now prevents trains from following so closely. Most of the water tanks and Grand Avenue station (middle of the view) are gone, and the area is emerging as a restaurant, condo loft office and residential area. Just completed in 1989, there is a new elevated structure on Wells Street (with clearance increased to avoid collision with the 14-foot highway trailers) and a modernized station for the Merchandise Mart, off the view to the right. *(All photos Krambles Collection)*

ABOVE: Where did Light Rail Transit (LRT) start its renaissance in the United States? Would you believe the Skokie Swift? This "demonstration project" was undertaken by CTA under the leadership of George Krambles in 1964, when federal government policy was about to undergo a metamorphosis. At that time, there was no public funding assistance, as there was for highway, waterway or aviation systems. This was one of the reasons why so many electric rail lines disappeared. In Chicago, earlier studies had been made of continuing service on part of the Chicago Aurora & Elgin Railway (to Lombard or Wheaton, using modified PCC streetcars) and on part of the Chicago North Shore & Milwaukee Railway (to Waukegan, using new CTA-like cars and A/B alternate stop service). Interurban operations predominantly in the rush direction would change to frequent two-way service. To implement either the CA&E or CNS&M replacement plans, sources of capital and operating subsidy funds were needed, but neither was available then. In 1962, a very modest program was launched in the U. S.—Housing and Home Finance Agency (HHFA)—to provide funding assistance for "service improvement experiments." HHFA projects in

Detroit (to double the frequency of bus service) and in Washington (to provide a low-cost bus shuttle in G Street in the central business district) were interesting but not too relevant to rail transits. The then-mayor of Skokie, Myron Greisdorf, approached Walter J. McCarter, then CTA's General Manager, seeking a restoration of rail service to Skokie, which had been abandoned by the North Shore Line in January, 1963. Given a fine new expressway through to downtown Chicago, why did Skokie still want rail service? Well, the highway might be good enough during off-peak hours, but, in rush hours, residents of Skokie were faced with trying to squeeze into the highway at about its maximum load point. McCarter ordered his planning staff to make a quick study. An approach evolved from the earlier CA&E and CNS&M studies: run a nonstop shuttle between Howard and Dempster with a basic 15-minute headway. This shuttle would require only two cars, and these cars would be from the experimental high-performance cars, Series #1-4. Since there was then no federal, state or local capital assistance program, CTA acquired the abandoned railroad infrastructure from the North Shore Line and allocated the cars from its spare list. The federal program advanced funding for rehabilitation at a minimal level and for a station and parking lot (the latter designed and built by the Village of Skokie). The project was an immediate success, due to the cooperative effort of CTA, Skokie, the Chicago Area Transportation Study, the Northeastern Illinois Planning Commission and HHFA. On April 20, 1964, the opening day, the line expected to generate about 1,500 rides per weekday actually carried 3,939 people. (Traffic

later leveled off between 6,000-7,000 riders.) The first schedule was scrapped in a matter of an hour. In addition to the four high-speed cars, two others were pulled from the Evanston pool to carry the people. When the parking lot gate failed under the unexpected heavy duty, the official HHFA representative collected the quarter fares in his hat. In 1965, the four prototype articulated cars acquired in 1947-1948 came into their own on the "Swift," due to their ability to handle a large passenger load. During 1965, cars 53 and 52 were recorded in Evanston at Chicago Avenue, a former streetcar route many years ago. The "artics" served until 1986, when all four units were retired to railway museums. PRECEDING PAGE TOP: In 1969, as prototypes for the next car order, CTA had new cars #1 to #4 equipped as test beds for high-performance trucks and propulsion packages. Three of these high-speed double-end cars were recorded south of Jarvis on the North-South elevated line. PRECEDING PAGE LEFT: To minimize investment for the two-year project life, an austere and simple station layout with a single tail track and spring switch sufficed at Dempster Street terminal of the Skokie Swift, as shown in this photo of February 28, 1966. During 1989, a modern station is being constructed for CTA under the leadership of the Village of Skokie with funding assistance provided by the Illinois Department of Transportation and the Urban Mass Transportation Administration. In 1959, CTA ordered 50 double-end cars, adaptable for conventional multiple-car trains or for one-man, single-unit operation. Originally assigned Logan Square-Congress-Douglas (West-Northwest route) service, they are better known for

service on Evanston, Skokie Swift and Ravenswood. As traffic grew on Skokie Swift, more of these single-unit cars were assigned to the service. One challenge in adopting these cars for Skokie service was that half of the route was powered with third rail and half with overhead catenary. The North Shore Line had used trolley poles for the latter, but with one-man crewing remote control roof-mounted power collection equipment that could be raised and lowered at speed was needed. At the time, however, a lightweight pantograph to reach the 23-foot high trolley wire was not commercially available. Undaunted, CTA shops came up with a pan trolley using a pair of ordinary trolley pole assemblies bridged at the top with a carbon-insert pantograph shoe and at an intermediate point by an airfoil (like a short airplane wing). The scheme worked out by MCERA's Bert Misek kept constant upward pressure against the wire at speeds up to 70 mph. A similar idea had been tested on an Illinois Terminal Railroad 240-class car in 1935, but, lacking the airfoil, it had been unsuccessful. ABOVE LEFT: During the Skokie Swift's first winter, a single car was northbound on the Oakton Street curve on January 26, 1965. *(All CTA photos from the Krambles Collection)* ABOVE RIGHT: During 1986, the Skokie Swift cars were part of a lot of 46 cars rehabilitated by Morrison-Knudsen. Eight cars were remanufactured into four, two-car units numbered 61-64. Car 39 is shown northbound on the Oakton Street curve on June 26, 1987. *(WDM)* Over the years, this line has enjoyed consistent growth in reverse commuter business due to the development in the suburbs.

The 1960's saw continued progress for CTA. Two orders of high-performance rolling stock were received. Construction started on the first new route in over 50 years and on a significant extension of another line, ending a cycle of branch line abandonments. TOP: A train of 2000-series cars, built by Pullman in 1964, was at the 95th Street station on the Dan Ryan line on November 4, 1971. The line had opened for service on September 28, 1969. In 1988, an expansion of the 98th Street yard neared completion in anticipation of through-routing the Dan Ryan and Howard lines. BOTTOM: In 1969, the Budd Company delivered 150 stainless steel cars of the 2200-series to the City of Chicago for use by CTA on its lines. The city also funded construction of the Dan Ryan line and extension of the Northwest line from Logan Square via a short subway and the median of the Kennedy Expressway to Jefferson Park station. This extension opened for service on February 1, 1970. This train of 2200's was photographed at Belmont, one stop beyond Logan Square, on March 30, 1970. The Kennedy line was extended from Jefferson Park to River Road on February 27, 1983, and from River Road to O'Hare International Airport on September 3, 1984. (*Two photos CTA, Krambles Collection*)

On October 6, 1976, the inaugural run of the 2400-series cars was operated from the Merchandise Mart. Sitting in the "railfan" seat on this trip was Mayor Richard J. Daley, accompanied by CTA Chairman, James McDonough, and General Manager, George Krambles. According to David Young's article in the *Chicago Tribune,* "The four stainless steel, $300,000 cars, built by Boeing-Vertol Company, roared down the Dan Ryan line toward 95th Street as the mayor smiled and judged the ride 'fine.'" These four cars were the prototype cars that would be subjected to a 600-hour in-service test before production deliveries would start on the remaining 196 cars. These 200 cars were the only rapid transit cars built by Boeing-Vertol Company. They are somewhat of an international car, as the car bodies were fabricated in Portugal while the trucks, motor-alternator sets and track brakes came from Germany. These cars were built under the supervision of Walter R. Keevil, now CERA's president and a long-time Board member. Walter is following in the footsteps of his uncle, the late Charles E. Keevil, who was Project Engineer for the introduction of 1500-v DC cars on the Chicago South Shore & South Bend Railroad in the middle 1920's and who influenced rapid transit car designs in the 6000-2000-2200 series era at CTA. ABOVE: Cars 2409 and 2410 were on a Ravenswood run at Diversey Avenue on August 16, 1977. The initial assignment for these cars was on the Ravenswood route, followed by assignment on the Howard-Jackson Park Englewood line. *(Walter R. Keevil photo)* LEFT: On June 26, 1987, a pair of 2400's led a southbound train at Madison and Wabash on Chicago's historic Loop on a Lake-Dan Ryan run. In 1988, the surviving cars of the series were all assigned to the Lake-Dan Ryan line. *(WDM)* CTA equipment is well photographed. FACING PAGE TOP: This scene at Wacker and Wells, with the Merchandise Mart—location of CTA's headquarters—in the background, is an example. New rapid transit cars and a new articulated bus from AM General were prepared to serve Chicago. Deliveries of the 2400's were completed in 1978. *(CTA photo Krambles*

Collection) RIGHT: The 2600-series cars are an evolution of the 2400-series cars. However, they are historic in at least two ways: They are the largest single order ever placed for rapid transit cars for Chicago (one purchase order—initially for 300 cars, with a change order to add an additional 300 cars) and they were the last cars to be built by the Budd Company and its successor, Transit America. The interiors, propulsion package, SCM camshaft control and many other features are quite similar to the 2400's. The car body is similar and the motorman was provided with, for the first time since the 5000-series cars, a dedicated cab and a better seat based on experience with prior car series. Other changes included sculptured fiber glass ends with the contours redesigned to reduce the gap between the cars at the train doors and a dedicated space for wheelchair passengers. The four prototypes were delivered in March, 1981. Production deliveries began in December, 1981, and continued to May, 1987, all under the project management of Walter Keevil. These cars permitted gradual phaseout of the 6000-series cars. On June 26, 1987, this train crossed the Chicago River at Wells Street. In 1989, 2601-3200-series cars serve on all routes except the Skokie Swift. *(WDM)*

LEFT: On June 26, 1987, a train of 2600's on a Ravenswood run leaves the Loop at Lake and Wells. BELOW: CTA's newest cars, some of which have been in service for less than one year at CTA's newest terminal, O'Hare Airport, are shown on June 27, 1987. O'Hare is now among the upper 10% of CTA stations on ridership generated! FACING PAGE: On the previous day, car 2744 led a Ravenswood train northbound around the curve at North Avenue and Sedgwick. What is ahead for the rapid transit? Ground breaking occurred in February, 1987, on the new nine-mile Southwest line which will connect with the existing system at 18th Street and Clark and which follows the Archer Avenue Corridor to Midway Airport, a $500 million project expected to open in 1993. Included in the project are the 3200-series rapid transit cars. CTA hopes to obtain between 230 to 250 of these cars, which will have corrugated sides below their hopper windows. These cars will complete the replacement of the 6000-series and provide rolling stock for the Southwest line. Meanwhile, renewal of the Howard Yard and interlocking continues as Chicago makes significant, but unfortunately insufficient, investment in its rapid transit system. (WDM)

In 1988, Boston has three heavy rapid transit lines, known as the Blue, Orange and Red lines. The Blue Line connects Bowdoin in downtown Boston with Wonderland in Revere. FACING PAGE: From June 22, 1875, to January 27, 1940, the Boston, Revere Beach & Lynn (BRB&L) operated a steam-powered narrow gauge line that was electrified in 1928. On its final day of service, this train entered the East Boston station and ferry terminal. *(C. L. Siebert, Jr.)* Meanwhile, streetcar service commenced in a subway from Maverick Square in East Boston to downtown on December 30, 1904. ABOVE: On April 21, 1924, the operation was converted to rapid transit service using this fleet of Pullman-built utilitarian cars. BELOW: On January 5, 1952, rapid transit service was extended to Orient Heights and on January 19, 1954, to Wonderland. The extension was built primarily on the abandoned BRB&L right-of-way. To serve this extension, 40 cars were delivered in 1951. On April 25, 1972, the "old" cars were photographed at Wonderland and the "new" cars at Orient Heights. *(Two photos Roy G. Benedict)* RIGHT: In 1979, the fleet of 70 "Bluebells" replaced the existing rolling stock. On October 10, 1982, this train was at the Government Center station (formerly Scollay Square). *(FWS)*

The Orange Line runs on a north-south axis through the central business section of Boston via the Washington Street subway—about the only part of the route that has not been changed in recent years. On June 10, 1901, service began from Sullivan Square in Charlestown to Dudley Square in Roxbury, passing through downtown via the Tremont Street subway. On November 30, 1908, the trains were rerouted through the paralleling Washington Street subway. Service was extended from Dudley to Forest Hills on November 22, 1909, and from Sullivan to Everett on March 15, 1919. This was described at the time as a "temporary" station, and the intended destination was to be Malden. LEFT: From 1957, cars built by Pullman-Standard utilizing PCC technology served on the Orange Line. On April 26, 1972, this train was at Sullivan Square. *(Roy G. Benedict)* BELOW: In 1980, the first of a new order of cars, nicknamed the "Orange Blossoms," entered service. Photo taken October 10, 1982, shows northbound train entering the Dudley Square station. *(FWS)* In the 1970's, a series of long-planned changes began on the Orange Line. The elevated portion of the route to Everett was finally replaced by a new line to Malden Square that opened

in four segments: Haymarket to Sullivan Square on April 4, 1975, and then one station at a time to Wellington on September 6, 1975, Malden Center on December 27, 1975, and Oak Grove on March 19, 1977. Next, the South Side elevated to Forest Hills was replaced as a part of a $743 million project, construction of which spanned eight years. In this project, the former New Haven Railroad right-of-way on an embankment was replaced by a concrete-lined trench that contains the two rapid transit tracks and three tracks for Amtrak's northeast corridor and MBTA's commuter rail operations. There are nine Orange Line stations on this 4.7-mile segment, which includes a 52-acre linear park. RIGHT: The new Forest Hills terminal is shown on November 28, 1987. BELOW: On the same day, an inbound train was at Roxbury Crossing. *(WDM)*

The Red Line, heavily patronized, traditionally connected Cambridge (Harvard Square) with Dorchester and the Ashmont-Mattapan "high-speed" trolley line. Its service was extended south to Quincy Center on September 1, 1977, to Braintree on March 22, 1980, and northward from Harvard Square to Davis Square on December 8, 1984, and on to Alewife on March 30, 1985. The line received new rolling stock as well. Pullman-Standard constructed 92 cars in the 01400-series in 1962 and 1963 and 76 cars in the 01500-series and 01600-series in 1969 and 1970. In 1987 and 1988, 60 cars in the 01700-series were received from the Canadian builder, UTDC. ABOVE: Representatives of the two Pullman-Standard orders were at Porter station on November 28, 1985. The 1969 "Silverbirds" outbound to Alewife were on the lower level while some 1963 "Redbirds" were inbound on the upper level. (WDM) LEFT: Shortly after entering service, car 01709 was at Cabot Yard on April 6, 1988. (Norton D. Clark) FACING PAGE: In their original blue and white livery, two of the 1963 cars crossed the Charles River on October 12, 1970. (FWS)

Rapid transit service in New York City dates from February 14, 1870, when a cable-operated line was opened. Steam power followed shortly thereafter, and between 1900 and 1903 the lines were electrified. ABOVE: In October, 1887, Gilbert & Bush delivered a series of trail cars to be pulled by steam locomotives over the New York City elevated system. In 1902 and 1903, these cars were electrified. The cars served on the 6th Avenue elevated until it was abandoned on December 4, 1938, and on the 9th Avenue and 2nd Avenue lines north of 60th Street until they were abandoned on June 13, 1940. The cars sat idle for a while but, during World War II, 90 of these cars were purchased by the U. S. Maritime Commission for use between Emeryville and Richmond, California, on the Shipyard Railway. This railway was operated by the Key System from January 18, 1943, to September 30, 1945. *(GK)* FACING PAGE: The major

divisions which comprised the New York City system are the former Brooklyn-Manhattan Transit Corporation (BMT), Independent Subway (IND), and the Interborough Rapid Transit Company (IRT). Upon unification in 1940, the system was called the Board of Transportation. On June 15, 1953, the New York City Transit Authority (TA) became the new operating agency. On March 1, 1968, the TA was absorbed by the Metropolitan Transportation Authority; however, the TA keeps a separate identity for its rapid transit operations. But there was still time for a little fun. Car 1316 with open platforms, shown here, traces its origin to the Brooklyn Rapid Transit Company. These cars, which were built in 1905 and 1906, were used until 1958 in daily service on the Myrtle Avenue elevated in Brooklyn and in Queens. For a fan trip on June 16, 1958, adhesive tape was used to simulate the lettering. *(Krambles Collection)*

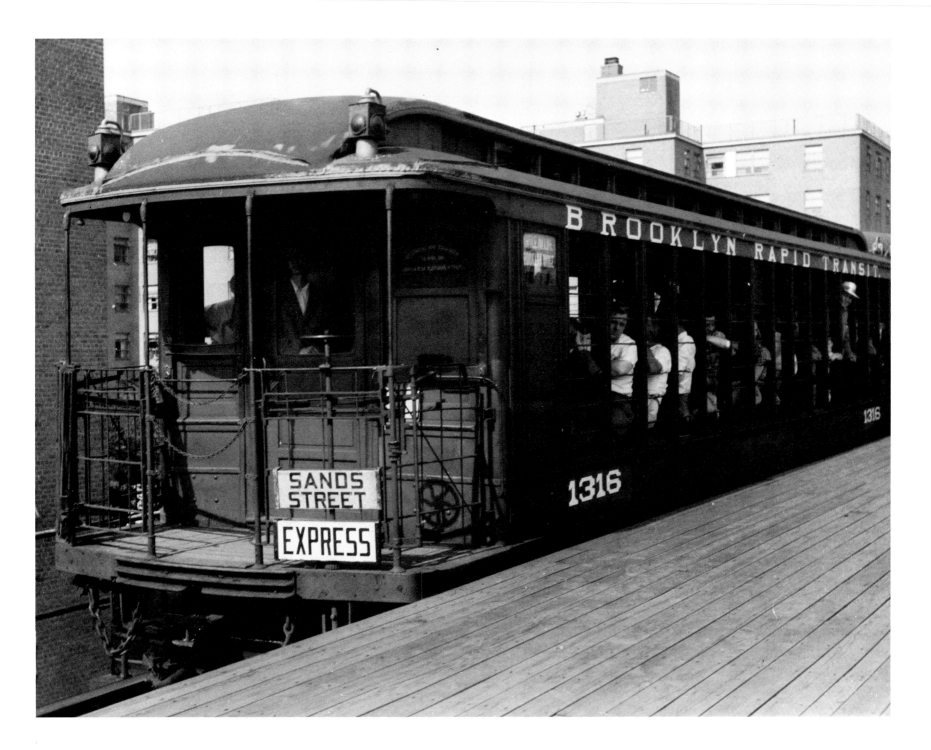

ABOVE: The "Q" cars of the Brooklyn Manhattan Transit (BMT) had an interesting history during CERA's early years. Built between 1903 and 1907, they were converted into three-car sets, painted blue with white and orange trim—the colors of the City of New York—for use in 1939 and 1940 as transportation to the World's Fair. The cars served on the Flushing and Astoria lines until 1949. In April, 1950, some of the "Q's" were transferred to the 3rd Avenue line in Manhattan. For this service, the trucks were changed, which raised the height of the cars. From December, 1956, to April, 1958, the cars were in storage. Then, they were transferred to the Myrtle Avenue elevated, but not until the roofs were lowered so the cars would fit in the Montague Street subway that

would become the access to the yards and shop at Coney Island when the new Christie Street subway was completed. At this time, the threshold extensions were added so that the cars could operate with platforms intended for the wide division cars. This single unit of three cars was photographed approaching the Sumner Avenue station in Brooklyn. LEFT: An interior view of a "Q" car. *(Two photos FWS)* TOP LEFT: BMT was willing to experiment with new equipment. It ordered the first PCC streetcars as well as the first PCC cars for rapid transit duty. This is BMT 8000, resplendent in its blue, ivory and Chinese red livery. The 8000 was delivered in 1938, followed by five more of these three-section articulated cars in 1940. Known as "Bluebirds," they were in service until 1957. *(Krambles Collection)* TOP RIGHT: North of the Harlem River in the Bronx at 238th Street, a southbound train on September 19, 1969, was on Line 1, the Broadway Local. BOTTOM RIGHT: Transit at sea: Trains to Rockaway Park and Far Rockaway on the A and CC lines crossed Jamaica Bay on this trestle. Originally, this service was provided by the Long Island Railroad. However, during the 1950's, the line was converted to a rapid transit operation, with service commencing to Rockaway Beach on June 28, 1956, and to Far Rockaway on January 16, 1958. Trains to this point also served 8th Avenue in Manhattan. *(Two photos FWS)*

The sheer size of NYCTA is startling: 41,000 employees, $1 billion in fares annually from riders, 6,200 transit cars and 3,800 buses, a $3 billion operating budget and a capital program between 1987 and 1991 of approximately $7 billion. FACING PAGE TOP LEFT: Now part of NYCTA, the Staten Island Rapid Transit was owned by the Baltimore & Ohio Railroad from 1899 to 1971. On March 26, 1967, cars 334 and 317 were recorded approaching Princess Bay station. In 1973, these cars were replaced by 52 cars of the R44 series. TOP RIGHT: A train of veterans was on the fabled 3rd Avenue elevated at 204th Street on April 1, 1967. This was the last elevated railway route in Manhattan. The first segment to go was from Chatham Square to City Hall on December 31, 1953. When the major segment from Chatham Square to 149th Street was abandoned on May 12, 1955, "all of New York," fans and nonfans alike, was out to ride and photograph the line. The final segment from 149th Street to Gun

Hill Road was closed on April 28, 1973. *(Two photos Roy G. Benedict)* BOTTOM: New York is famous for its elevated junctions. This is Broadway Junction in the East New York district of Brooklyn on August 1, 1976. The "J" train, led by R7A-class car 1596, was a Jamaica Express on the Broadway-Brooklyn-Fulton line. The Canarsie line and Fulton Street (8th Avenue) line (to Far Rockaway) crossed in this area. ABOVE: Serving on a Flushing Line train, R-36 cars built by St. Louis Car Co. for the 1964-1965 World's Fair still displayed their blue and white paint scheme on June 15, 1970, as the train passed near Sunnyside Yard. On December 11, 1988, the long-awaited Archer Avenue subway opened in southeast Queens. Two stations and the terminal, Jamaica Center, at Archer Avenue and Parsons Boulevard, the first new stations in 20 years, opened with the line. Service changes affected nine routes and affected all boroughs except Richmond (Staten Island). *(Two photos FWS)*

109

What is known today as PATH was for years a joint operation of the Hudson & Manhattan and the Pennsylvania Railroad. The service connects Newark, Jersey City and Hoboken, New Jersey, with two terminals, 33rd Street and World Trade Center, in Manhattan, New York City. FACING PAGE: Car 285 dates from 1909. On April 2, 1946, it led this eastbound train at Journal Square in Jersey City. These cars served into the 1960's. *(Thomas H. Desnoyers photo from Krambles Collection)* BELOW: The Pennsylvania Railroad was responsible for providing a portion of the rolling stock. In 1958, St. Louis Car Co. delivered the 50 K-class cars. The Pennsylvania Railroad, which owned most of the trackage west of Journal Square, acquired 30 of these cars. This train was en route to Newark. *(Bruce C. Bente photo)* RIGHT: PATH took over on September 1, 1962, at a time of much need for new equipment and facilities. Some new rolling stock arrived in 1965, with additional cars arriving in 1967 and 1972. Known as PA cars, they replaced the original fleet. On September 19, 1969, two-year-old car 712 headed this train into the Harrison station. *(FWS)* In 1988, an $850 million rehabilitation program is in progress which includes a new maintenance shop and yard, power distribution improvements, major rehabilitation of stations, rehabilitation of 247 PA cars and delivery of 95 new PA-4 cars built by Kawasaki. These cars will allow for retirement of the "K-cars" and provide additional needed capacity.

September 18, 1938. Service on the north end was extended to Fern Rock on September 9, 1956, and, to serve the region's major sports facilities, south to Pattison Avenue on April 6, 1973. LEFT: The Broad Street line was served by two groups of cars built in 1928 and 1938, respectively. On October 14, 1956, a train of the 1938 cars was recorded entering the subway at Fern Rock. *(John J. Bowman)* BELOW: Replacements for the original fleet arrived in 1981 and 1982 in the form of 125 stainless steel cars built by Kawasaki Heavy Industries. The order included 76 single-end cars and 49 double-end cars. Up to eight cars can be operated in a train. In October, 1987, a train of the new cars left Fern Rock. At the same time as the new cars were received, stations on the line were modernized. *(FWS)*

Philadelphia is served by three rapid transit lines, two of which are operated by the Southeastern Pennsylvania Transportation Authority (SEPTA) and the third by Port Authority Transit Corporation (PATCO). On these pages, we visit the two lines operated by SEPTA, the Market-Frankford and Broad Street lines, which cross under City Hall in downtown Philadelphia. The Market Street line began operations from 69th Street east to 15th Street on March 4, 1907, and was extended eastward during 1908 through downtown. The line on to Frankford was not completed until November 5, 1922. FACING PAGE TOP: On March 5, 1950, cars 550, 516 and 512 made up a train on the Frankford elevated. These cars were part of a group of 100 cars delivered in 1922 for the opening of the Frankford elevated. Together with 215 Market Street cars built between 1906 and 1913, they served until 1960. (John J. Bowman, Jr.) BOTTOM: On May 27, 1960, the Budd Company delivered the first of 270 new cars. They were the first production run of stainless steel rapid transit cars built in the United States. The higher running speeds of these new cars reduced the trip time from 45 to 35 minutes. *(FWS)* In 1988, the elevated structure on the Frankford portion of the line is undergoing major rehabilitation. Service on the Broad Street line between City Hall and Olney Street commenced on September 2, 1928. It was extended south to South Avenue on April 20, 1930, and to Snyder Avenue on

On June 7, 1936, the Delaware River Bridge Line began operation between 8th and Market in Philadelphia and Broadway Station in Camden over what is now known as the Benjamin Franklin Bridge. On January 4, 1969, this operation was taken over by Port Authority Transit Corporation (PATCO), which extended from Camden to Lindenwold, New Jersey. PATCO is a high-speed, high-tech line with automatic train operation, closed-circuit TV monitoring of station areas and automatic fare collection. Service is provided by 75 cars built by Budd in 1968 and 46 cars built by Canadian Vickers in 1980 and 1981. LEFT: On October 21, 1972, an outbound train was at Center Tower in Camden. BOTTOM LEFT: One of the new Canadian Vickers cars was westbound on leaving Woodcrest station on October 13, 1980, shortly after this car was delivered to PATCO. The trip from Lindenwold to 16th and Market in Philadelphia is 14.5 miles, and the rolling stock could attain 75 mph. BELOW: A two-car train was westbound between Lindenwold and Ashland stations on October 11, 1971. (All FWS)

The Mass Transit Administration, a department of the State of Maryland, began revenue service on November 21, 1983, over Baltimore Metro's 7.55 miles from Charles Center in downtown Baltimore northwest to Reistestown Plaza. On July 20, 1987, a six-mile extension was opened to Owings Mills. RIGHT: Cold Spring Station is on the original section, where this train was stopping on March 28, 1986. (WDM) Considerable design and engineering were needed for this section. The line starts at sea level and rises to an elevation of 450 feet. From Charles Center to Upton, deep tunnel construction was used in the soft ground.

Slurry wall construction was used here (as on Boston's new Orange Line to Forest Hills) because of proximity to sea level and the water table. Slurry wall construction is placing reinforced concrete in a trench excavation that is stabilized by a mixture of water and bentonite clay. From Upton to Mondawmin station, deep tunneling through hard rock was employed. The tunnels had to be relatively deep to pass under the Northeast Corridor (Amtrak, nee Pennsylvania Railroad) and CSX Transportation (nee B&O) tracks. BOTTOM RIGHT: The entire extension is at or above ground level. On October 24, 1987, a "short turn" trip was in the pocket track just north of Milford Mills station in Pikesville, Maryland. The CSXT train was westbound. BOTTOM LEFT: A portion of the extension was in the median of a new expressway. Shortly after the line opened, this train was between Owings Mills and Old Court stations. The rolling stock was built by the Budd Company and was nearly identical to the cars used on Miami's new rapid transit line. The fleet of 100 cars was delivered in two lots—72 cars in 1984 and 28 cars in 1986. All are equipped for automatic train operation. *(Two photos FWS)* The project cost to date is virtually $1 billion. Engineering is in progress to extend the line 1.5 miles from Charles Center to Johns Hopkins Hospital in east Baltimore at a cost of $327 million. A separate project, the first phase of which is budgeted at $240 million, is to provide a 22-mile light rail line from Timonium on the north to Dorsey on the south through the heart of Baltimore.

On March 27, 1976, the Washington Metropolitan Area Transit Authority (WMATA) commenced operations of its rapid transit system, commonly known as Metrorail. LEFT: Banners, flags and much public celebration heralded the long-awaited system. Washington had endured the detours, dust and planked roads for streets for years. BOTTOM RIGHT: Ceremonies were held at Rhode Island Avenue of the Red Line and the traditional free rides were offered. The crowd of people was trying to get on the trains, but those on the trains kept riding and riding. BOTTOM LEFT: The initial service was offered from Rhode Island Avenue to Farragut North, connecting Union Station, some government offices and the central business district. What developed was a lunch hour rush as people used Metrorail to travel to and from the central business district. This train shown was at Judiciary Square on opening day. Between 1976 and 1988, the system had grown by 70 miles and 64 stations, which represented a public investment approaching $7 billion. Rolling stock, all of which are equipped for automatic train operation, consist of 300 cars in the 1000-series built by Rohr Industries in 1974 and 1975, 71 cars in the 2000-series built by Breda in 1983 and 1984 and 290 cars of the 3000-series from Breda built from 1984 and continuing into 1989. Final assembly of the Breda cars was done by Amtrak at its Beech Grove shops. On its 10th birthday, Metrorail reflected on what had happened in the past decade: approximately 500,000 average weekday riders and combined annual bus-rail ridership of 216.2 million in 1986 versus 126.8 million

in 1976. About $3 billion of private real estate development has already taken place adjacent to the WMATA Metrorail routes. RIGHT: On July 1, 1977, the Blue Line opened from the Stadium-Armory station on a circuitous route past government buildings, through the central business district, across and then along the Potomac River past Rosslyn, Arlington National Cemetery and the Pentagon to National Airport. On November 11, 1977, this train was at Rosslyn. BELOW: National Airport has been the terminal of the Blue Line since it opened in 1977. *(All photos FWS)* In 1988, the Red Line extends 26.5 miles in a "U" shape from Shady Grove to Silver Springs, Maryland, via the central business district of Washington, D.C. An extension from Silver Springs to Wheaton is under construction and scheduled to open in late 1990. Ultimately, the line may extend one more station to Glenmont. The Orange Line extends 26.1 miles in an east-west axis from New Carrollton, Maryland, to Vienna,

Virginia. TOP LEFT: On April 19, 1980, a Blue Line train was at Arlington Cemetery en route to National Airport. TOP RIGHT: An eastbound Orange Line train crossed over Conrail trackage at Landover, Maryland, on October 27, 1979. It is at this point where the Conrail trackage joins Amtrak's Northeast Corridor. This Conrail trackage was the original Pennsylvania Railroad line into the District. It is now used to route freight trains around Union Station and connects with the trackage through Union Station in the vicinity of L'Enfant Plaza en route to Potomac Yard. The Orange Line parallels this Conrail trackage to its junction point with the Blue Line near Benning Road near the site of Capital Traction's Benning carhouse. BOTTOM: On October 27, 1979, an eastbound Orange Line train passed John F. Kennedy Stadium, home of the Washington Redskins, the 1988 Super Bowl champions. In 1988, the day Washington celebrated this victory, Metrorail achieved a new milestone in ridership—565,000 passengers for a single day! *(All photos WDM)*

The Metropolitan Atlanta Rapid Transit Authority (MARTA) was created in 1965. The rail system was approved by the voters in 1971. MARTA began rail operations in 1979 when 6.7 miles of the east-west line opened between Avondale and Georgia State stations on June 30 and when 5.1 miles to the west from Georgia State to Hightower opened on December 22. The north-south line, which intersects the east-west line at Five Points station, was opened in segments, beginning with the segment between Garnett and North Avenue opening on December 4, 1981. Additional segments were opened in 1982 and 1984, with Chamblee on the north being reached in December, 1987, and Hartsfield International Airport being opened on June 18, 1988. Construction continued on the North line to Doraville and the Proctor Creek Branch off the West line. Rolling stock consisted of 120 aluminum cars built by Franco Belge in 1979-1981 and 120 stainless steel cars built by Hitachi in 1984-1987. All were equipped for automatic train operation. ABOVE: An eastbound train entered the Georgia State station on the East line. TOP RIGHT: A northbound train was at Peachtree station on the North line. BOTTOM RIGHT: A train arrived at the Hightower terminal on the West line. All of these photographs were taken on October 10, 1984. *(WDM)*

Cleveland's rapid transit was planned from the 1920's, when Oris P. and Mantis J. Van Sweringen conceived the Union Terminal project and moved their Shaker Heights service from the streets of East Cleveland to private right-of-way from Union Terminal to Shaker Square. The initial segments of the rapid transit line were opened east from Union Terminal to Windermere on March 15, 1955, and west from Union Terminal to 117th Street on August 15, 1955. Two extensions on the west line, first to West Park on November 15, 1958, and the second from West Park on November 21, 1968, brought the line into Cleveland Hopkins International Airport, the first rapid transit line to reach an airport. Since 1955, the line has been served by three sets of rolling stock. ABOVE: The original cars were built by St. Louis Car Co. in 1954. There were 12 single-unit cars in the 100 series, like car 106, shown at East 79th Street on April 29, 1966, and 56 cars in married pairs. TOP RIGHT: In 1967, Pullman-Standard delivered 20 of these stainless steel cars, followed by 10 more cars in 1970. The design was influenced by Toronto's recently delivered cars, and the fiber glass ends evolved from the design for the Chicago Transit Authority's 2000-series cars of 1964. On August 20, 1977, car 174 was recorded at East 34th Street. Between Terminal Tower and East 65th Street, the trackage is shared with the Shaker Heights service, an interesting blurring of the definitions of rapid transit and light rail. *(Two photos Roy G. Benedict)* BOTTOM RIGHT: Replacement of the fleet came in 1983 and 1984 when 60 new stainless steel cars were delivered to the Greater Cleveland Regional Transit Authority by Tokyu Car Corporation. On January 11, 1986, car 196 was photographed at the Airport station. *(WDM)*

Toronto is the most vivid example of the impact on real estate development created by a rapid transit system. ABOVE: Compare this view of the Yonge line looking toward Eglinton Avenue from Davisville taken on July 6, 1969, with the adjacent photograph. *(FWS)* TOP RIGHT: The same view on August 24, 1984, documents the extensive real estate development. *(WDM)* Since 1954, investment has totaled $10 billion along the north-south Yonge-University-Spadina line and $20 billion along the east-west Bloor-Danforth line. The Yonge line opened on March 30, 1954, between Eglinton and Union Station, with 100 of these distinguished looking cars built by Gloucester Railway Carriage & Wagon Co. of England. These cars have been described as "regal" due to the wine-red color with gold trim, left-hand drive, heavyweight construction and cushioned seating. Subsequent cars were built with aluminum to reduce weight. In 1988, the Gloucester cars are scheduled to be replaced. BOTTOM RIGHT: Extensions of the line north on the University and Spadina axis and farther north on Yonge in 1963, 1973, 1974 and 1978 have created a "U"-shaped line that is 18.6 miles long. On July 1, 1984, the train shown was northbound in the W. R. Allen Expressway leaving the Lawrence West Station in the City of North York for the terminal at Wilson. *(FWS)*

The original segment of the Bloor-Danforth line opened between Keele and Woodbine on February 26, 1966. Subsequent extensions, both east and west in 1968 and 1980, have resulted in a 16.8-mile line between Islington and Kennedy. ABOVE: On August 25, 1984, an eastbound train was recorded leaving Old Mill station on the west end of the line, about to 'cross the Humber River. *(WDM)* TOP RIGHT: On June 23, 1969, two trains passed between Firvalley Court and Warden stations on the far east end of the line. Most of the rolling stock on this line was built by Hawker-Siddeley between 1965 and 1979. *(FWS)* BOTTOM RIGHT: On March 23, 1985, operation began on the 3.2-mile line. Scarborough RT began using UTDC's linear motor Intermediate Capacity Transportation System (ICTS) technology. On June 3, 1985, fully automated operation began. These two trains were at Lawrence East station on August 24, 1984. This service connects McCowan station with the Bloor-Danforth line at Kennedy. *(WDM)*

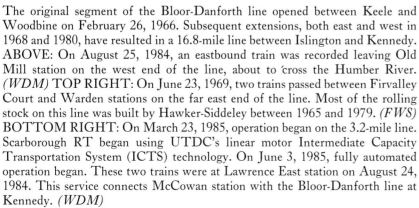

Day one for the Bay Area Rapid Transit (BART) District was September 11, 1972. BART was supposed to be the ultimate in rapid transit technology (using totally automated operation, including fare collection). Debugging took a considerable number of years. Despite considerable controversy, the system provided a much-needed service, as congestion on the Oakland Bay Bridge is prevalent for more hours of the day with each passing year. BART is a 75-mile system connecting Richmond on the north, Concord on the east and Fremont on the south in the East Bay area with San Francisco and Daly City on the peninsula. The operating center of BART is in Oakland at 12th Street. This is one of those coincidences of history. BART is a reincarnation of the Key System, Southern Pacific's Interurban Electric and the Sacramento Northern

Railway. What was suburban and interurban service of the 1920's and 1930's is rapid transit of the 1970's and beyond. 12th Street in downtown Oakland was an important point on the Key System. BART's Fruitvale station is one block from the site of the former SP Fruitvale station. BART uses the former SN right-of-way through Walnut Creek and Concord. As for a rail service connecting Oakland and Hayward, well, in 1892, there was the narrow-gauge Oakland, San Leandro & Hayward Electric Railway. BART's initial fleet of rolling stock included 350 cars—250 "A" cars with streamlined cabs at one end and 100 "B" cars that have no cabs, all built by Rohr Industries between 1971 and 1974. ABOVE: On July 5, 1977, 10-car Daly City to Concord train was east of Orinda station in the Oakland Hills. *(FWS)*

TOP LEFT: A westbound train was at Orinda station on July 1, 1977. BOTTOM LEFT: In the southern part of San Francisco, a Daly City train was between Balboa Park and Daly City on July 4, 1977. *(Two photos FWS)* ABOVE: A westbound train descended into the Trans Bay tube in Oakland on April 2, 1976. FACING PAGE: Beginning in 1987, BART began receiving the first of 150 "C" cars from Alsthom-Atlantique of France. The cars were BART's first to have cabs and yet be capable of midtrain placement. On July 19, 1988, a "C" car led a train between Union City and Fremont. *(FWS)* In 1988, work is under way to create more capacity at Daly City and a new station, the first in San Mateo County. Ultimately, this line is to be extended through South San Francisco to the airport. In the nearer term, extensions are planned from Concord to West Pittsburg, Fremont to Warm Springs and a branch off the Fremont line from the Bayfair station to the Dublin/Pleasanton area.

CHAPTER 4

MAIN LINE ELECTRIFICATION.... PROMISE DENIED

In 1938 the United States led the world in railroad electrification. From the time of the great eastern electrification projects that began shortly after the turn of the century, U.S. railroads had held a substantial lead over any other country in the application of electric traction to main line railroad transportation. By 1931, when American railroads were operating nearly 5,000 electrified track-miles, U.S. electrification represented nearly 20 percent of the world total and far more than any other country.

The capstone of main line electrification in the U.S. was the great Pennsylvania Railroad program for electrification of its eastern lines that was carried out during the 1930's. Initiated in the mid 1910's, the PRR program had extended 11,000 volt, single-phase, 25-cycle A.C. catenary over the system's multiple track main lines between New York and Washington by 1935. Early in 1937 the Pennsylvania's directors voted to extend electrification west to Harrisburg, and with the exuberant arrival of GG1 No. 4863 at Harrisburg leading the westbound *Metropolitan* on January 15, 1938, the triumph of U.S. electrification was complete. With some 7,000 track-miles of electric operation, U.S. railroads were the undisputed world leaders.

American electrification had gotten its start in the mid-1890's with a series of pioneering projects which had demonstrated the ability of the new technology of electric traction to handle main line railroad traffic. From 1895 onward, both the Pennsylvania and the New Haven railroads had developed a series of experimental branch line electrifications that employed low voltage D.C. power supply systems comparable to those being developed for street, interurban and rapid transit railway applications. But far and away the most important of these early projects had been the Baltimore & Ohio's electrification of some 3.6 miles of line at Baltimore, where D.C. locomotives successfully began hauling heavy main line passenger and freight trains through the Howard Street tunnel in 1895.

Main line electrification in the U.S. began in a big way soon after the turn of the century with a series of major projects in the San Francisco, New York and Philadelphia areas, all of which employed a D.C. third rail technology comparable to that adopted by the new rapid transit systems at Boston, New York, Philadelphia, and Chicago. The earliest of these was an electrification of the San Francisco Bay Area's North Shore Railroad, which installed a third rail D.C. system on its formerly narrow gauge suburban lines in Marin County in 1903. Over the period 1906-1913, in conjunction with its development of the new Grand Central Terminal in Manhattan, the New York Central & Hudson River carried out a major electrification program for both main line and suburban trains entering the city over its lines from the north. At the same time, the Pennsylvania Railroad completed major electrification projects for the new Hudson and East River tunnel lines into the railroad's new Pennsylvania Station on Manhattan, as well as an extensive electrification of the principal western Long Island suburban routes of its newly-acquired subsidiary, the Long Island Rail Road, which reached Pennsylvania Station through the new East River tunnel. In southern New Jersey, the Pennsylvania carried out another major D.C. third rail electrification on its West Jersey & Seashore subsidiary between Camden and Atlantic City.

The New York Central's New York project was quickly followed by the adoption of an identical system for electrification of the system's new Detroit River Tunnel in 1910. Still another early low voltage D.C. installation was made by the Niagara Junction, a Niagara Falls area switching line, which completed a 660 volt D.C. system in 1913.

While these early D.C. installations worked well enough for the relatively short distances involved, the heavy current flows required—and the concurrent voltage drop—made low voltage D.C. a poor choice for the heavy power demands of main line railroad operation over longer distances, and other electrification technologies soon came to the forefront.

Even as the major D.C. electrifications at New York were being installed by the New York Central and the Pennsylvania, high voltage A.C. electrification was being pioneered by the New York, New Haven & Hartford. In 1905 the New Haven began an 11,000 volt, single-phase, 25-cycle electrification of its main line out of New York that ultimately extended all the way to New Haven, Connecticut, together with two principal commuter branches in Connecticut.

Based upon the New Haven's success, similar A.C. electrifications were widely employed for a number of subsequent projects. The Boston & Maine used the 11,000 volt, single-phase, 25-cycle system for its 1911 electrification of the Hoosac Tunnel. Soon afterward the Norfolk & Western adopted the same system for an electrification of some 209 miles of mountainous West Virginia lines completed over a ten-year period from 1915 to 1924. In 1925 the parallel Virginian completed an even longer mountain electrification with an identical A.C. system.

Despite its initial experience with low voltage D.C., the Pennsylvania Railroad, too, adopted the 11,000 volt, 25-cycle system when it began the electrification of suburban lines out of Philadelphia in 1915. Eventually, the Pennsy's A.C. system extended all the way from New York to Washington, and from Philadelphia to Harrisburg. The Reading Company became another convert to 11,000 volt, 25-cycle A.C. when it electrified principal suburban routes out of its Philadelphia terminal in 1931.

If 11,000 volts, single-phase, 25-cycle power became a near standard for early A.C. electrification, there were a number of interesting variations as well. In 1909, the Great Northern electrified its Cascade Tunnel with a novel 6600-volt, three-phase, 25-cycle A.C. system, although this was replaced with the 11,000 volt, single-phase, 25-cycle system during 1927-29, concurrent with completion of the new Cascade Tunnel. In 1908, Canada's Grand Trunk Railway electrified the St. Clair Tunnel between Port Huron, Michigan, and Sarnia, Ontario, with a 3300-volt, single-phase, 25 cycle A.C. system. Henry Ford's Detroit, Toledo & Ironton completed a short-lived 22,000 volt, single-phase, 25-cycle A.C. electrification in 1926, and in 1929 the Pacific Electric Railway of Costa Rica opened a 79-mile electrification that employed a

unique—to North America at least—15,000 volt, single-phase, 20 cycle A.C. system.

A strong rival to A.C. electrification was the high-voltage D.C. system developed by the General Electric Company. GE had installed a 1200 volt D.C. system on an Indiana interurban as early as 1907, and within a few years 1200- or 1500-volt D.C. systems were virtually standard for new interurban railways. So long as a low D.C. voltage was used, the heavy power demands of main line railroads had made the use of a third rail system mandatory. But by reducing both the size of power feeders and the number of substations required, the high voltage D.C. system made overhead power distribution and long distance installations practical for D.C. electrification of main line railroads.

The first high voltage D.C. installation for a railroad was a suburban service electrification of Southern Pacific lines out of Oakland, California, completed in 1911 with a 1200-volt system. Two years later GE completed a major 2400-volt D.C. electrification for the Butte, Anaconda & Pacific, a Montana copper ore carrier, which represented a showcase for the application of the new technology to heavy main line traffic demands. The success of the BA&P installation led to the adoption of a 3000-volt D.C. system for the Chicago, Milwaukee, St. Paul & Pacific, the longest of all American electrifications.

Completed over a 13-year period from 1915 to 1927, the Milwaukee electrification eventually comprised a total of some 663 route-miles on two separate sections in Montana, Idaho, and Washington.

At Montreal, the Canadian Northern adopted a 2400-volt D.C. system for a Mt. Royal Tunnel electrification opened in 1918, while the Montreal Harbour Commission employed the same system for an extensive electrification of harbor area switching lines completed in 1922. The Mexican Railway adopted the 3000-volt D.C. system for an electrification completed during 1924-28 that conquered severe mountain grades on its Mexico City-Veracruz main line. The same system was the choice for a smoke abatement electrification of the Cleveland Union Terminal opened in 1930, as well as a major electrification of Delaware, Lackawanna & Western suburban lines radiating from Hoboken, New Jersey, that was completed during 1930-31. An electrification of the Illinois Central's Chicago suburban services that opened in 1926 used a 1500-volt system similar to the earlier Southern Pacific installation in the West Side area of Portland, Oregon.

Even after the ascendancy of single-phase A.C. and high voltage D.C. electrification technologies, there were a few later installations carried out with the original low voltage D.C. system. In 1925 the B&O's Staten Island Rapid Transit Railway completed an electrification of its suburban lines with a D.C. third rail system identical to that of the New York subway system, largely because of plans for a tunnel across the New York Narrows that would eventually link SIRT with the subway in Brooklyn. Another late example of low voltage D.C. technology was the 1927 electrification of the 3-foot-gauge Boston, Revere Beach & Lynn, which employed a 600-volt D.C. overhead system.

In 1938 American railroads seemed poised on the threshold of a new era of main line electrification. Only two years before, the Federal Power Commission had released a report which suggested that electrification of an additional 12,000 miles of track on 20 railroads was economically feasible. Indeed, the arguments for electrification, amply demonstrated by the projects already operating, seemed compelling in the extreme. Electric operation reduced running times and increased tonnage capacity. Fuel costs were much lower with electric power than any other form of motive power. Maintenance costs for electric locomotives were a fraction of those for steam power, their availability was two to three times greater, and their economic lives promised to be twice as long as steam locomotives. In many cases the savings realized from electric operation were sufficient to repay the cost of electrification in as little as five years.

Yet, for all that, the 7000 track-miles of U.S. electrification in 1938—scarcely 2 percent of the U.S. total—was to represent the zenith of American electrification. The reasons for electrification's disappointing failure to achieve its full potential were many.

One problem throughout the early history of electric traction had been the failure to standardize. While A.C. electrification at least settled on the 11,000 volt, single-phase, 25-cycle system, D.C.

electrification came with both third rail and overhead distribution systems, and voltages that ranged from 600 to 3000 volts. Even within the basic systems there was a lack of uniform standards for electrical installations and equipment.

But electrification's greatest handicap was its enormous capital cost; despite the potential savings in operating costs, most railroads were simply unable to raise the needed capital. This had become a particular problem during the depression 1930's, when traffic levels and earnings were way down. Even the great Pennsylvania Railroad was able to complete its massive eastern electrification only on the strength of Reconstruction Finance Corporation (RFC) and Works Progress Administration (WPA) loans. By the time traffic began to pick up again in the late 1930's, World War II intervened to set aside any plans for additional electrification.

If additional electrification was frustrated by the depression and the war, there were some important advances in electric motive power during the late 1930's and the 1940's. In 1931 General Electric had developed ten highly successful EP-3 class high-speed, 2-C+C-2 locomotives for the New Haven electrification. These were followed in 1938 and 1942-43 by a further 16 streamlined EP-4 and EF-3 locomotives of similar design for high speed passenger and freight operations.

Tests with one of the New Haven's EP-3's in 1933 led the Pennsylvania Railroad to the development of a prototype GG1 locomotive with an identical 2-C+C-2 wheel arrangement. The streamlined GG1 was almost 80 feet long, weighed more than 230 tons, and was capable of a short-term output of 8500 h.p. In tests conducted late in 1934 the prototype reached speeds as high as 115 m.p.h., and proved to have markedly superior tracking abilities over the rigid frame designs previously favored by the Pennsylvania. An additional 57 GG1's were promptly ordered, and by the time production of this exceptional electric locomotive ended in 1943, the Pennsy had acquired a total of 139 GG1's.

Paced by the GG1, the Pennsylvania's eastern electrification helped to write one of the greatest chapters in the history of American railroading. The GG1's great power and speed permitted them to make the New York-Washington run with 20-car trains in as little as 3 hours 35 minutes, averaging an overall speed of more than a mile-a-minute despite half a dozen intermediate stops. Between Philadelphia and New York, the big electric made the 90-mile run, with three intermediate stops, in as little as 94 minutes.

Electrification permitted the Pennsy to accommodate with relative ease a staggering wartime traffic that would simply have been impossible to handle with steam. Freight traffic on the PRR's electric lines climbed some 40 percent above pre-Great Depression levels. The 1944 electrified freight traffic reached a record level of 18 million gross ton miles. Passenger volume, too, rose to prodigious levels. On the peak wartime day - Christmas Eve 1943 - electric trains carried some 179,000 passengers on the New York-Washington line, more than two-and-a-half-times the greatest single-day traffic in pre-war years. Quite simply, electrification made it possible for the Pennsylvania to keep its wartime traffic moving in support of the war effort.

In the immediate post-war years the General Electric Company's Erie (Pennsylvania) works produced some notable electric locomotive designs in support of modernization and increased traffic needs on several of the original electrifications. The first of these to appear were two W-1 class streamlined B-D + D-B units acquired to supplement the original motive power on the Great Northern's Cascade Tunnel electrification. Each of the 101-foot, 360-ton motor-generator units was capable of a continuous output of 5000 h.p. and a starting tractive effort of 180,000 pounds. Capable of exceeding the pulling power of even a Union Pacific "Big Boy" by a third, they were the most powerful single-unit electrics in the world.

A year later GE built four even more powerful streamlined motor-generator electrics for the Virginian electrification. Each of these EL-2B units was made up of two semi-permanently coupled cab units extending over 150 feet between coupler faces and weighing about 517 tons. With a rating of 6800 h.p. and a starting tractive effort of 260,000 pounds, the EL-2B's were billed as the most powerful continuous rated locomotives in the world.

In 1950 the Milwaukee Road took possession of a dozen big 2-D + D-2 GE units that had a most uncommon history. The big D.C. units had been part of an order for 20 locomotives for the Soviet Union placed in 1946. Before the big electrics were completed deteriorating East-West relations had blocked shipment, but GE finished the order anyway and began looking for alternate buyers.

Three were sold to the Chicago South Shore & South Bend, while five eventually went to Brazil's Paulista Railway. The balance of the "Little Joes," as they became known, went to the Milwaukee Road's western electrification. Each of the 89-foot, 273-ton units delivered a continuous rating of 5500 h.p. and a starting tractive effort of almost 111,000 pounds. Capable of multiple unit operations, they added an extraordinary pulling capacity to the Milwaukee's electric motive power roster.

In the immediate post-war years, too, there were some important technological developments that promised to make main line electrification more attractive than ever. Chief among these was the development of a practical rectifier for locomotive use. Capable of converting A.C. power to D.C., the rectifier made it possible to combine the efficiencies of high voltage, single phase A.C. power distribution with the traction efficiencies of the low-voltage D.C. series motor. And because low-frequency A.C. power was no longer needed for the large single-phase motors used in previous A.C. electrifications, the rectifier made it possible to electrify with 60-cycle power directly from the commercial grid, eliminating the substantial investment in substations, conversion equipment, and separate transmission lines that had been necessary for earlier A.C. electrifications.

Although rectifiers had been available for years, it was not until the late 1940's that designs had been developed that made them rugged enough to be practical for railroad motive power. In 1949 the Pennsylvania experimented successfully with a rectifier-equipped M.U. car. This was followed two years later with a pair of experimental Westinghouse rectifier freight locomotives, which operated extensively on both the Pennsylvania and New Haven electrifications.

The earliest U.S. production applications of the new rectifier technology were for new equipment for the existing electrifications, rather than new installations of electric traction. The New Haven was the first to take advantage of the new motive power technology. In 1954 the company placed an order for a fleet of 100 ignitron-rectifier M.U. cars for its New York suburban services, followed a year later by an order for ten 4000 h.p. GE passenger locomotives. Several years later the Virginian followed with an order for a dozen GE-built, 3300 h.p. ignitron-rectifier units that employed a road-switcher configuration comparable to that which had become a near standard for diesel-electric motive power.

By far the largest application of the new rectifier technology was by the Pennsylvania Railroad. Six prototype rectifier M.U. cars delivered by the Budd Company in 1958 were to be followed in the 1960's by major orders for similar equipment that permitted the Pennsy to begin the replacement of its aging original fleet of MP54 M.U. cars. In 1959 the Pennsylvania made a major commitment to rectifier motive power when it concluded a long-term lease agreement with General Electric for the provision of a $32 million fleet of 66 E44 locomotives that would replace the railroad's 93 P5a freight units that dated from the early 1930's. Essentially an upgraded version of GE's Virginian rectifier unit, the E44 was a 193-ton, 4400 h.p. locomotive capable of a maximum starting tractive effort of 89,000 pounds.

Despite the even greater potential advantages of electric traction with the advent of the new rectifier technology and commercial frequency electrification, new main line electrifications failed to appear in the post-war years, even though there seemed to be no shortage of likely candidates.

For some railroads, cost and a shortage of capital seemed to continue to be the problem. The Pennsylvania, for example, had been considering the electrification of its main line across the Pennsylvania mountains to Pittsburgh as early as 1930. The project was put off first by the Depression, and then by World War II. At war's end the electrification studies were updated again, and the two principal electrical manufacturers were developing plans for a new fleet of PRR electrics for service between Harrisburg and Pittsburgh. But after the war the railroad's finances were no longer healthy enough to take on the enormous cost of further electrification. Instead, the Pennsylvania began the dieselization of its non-electrified lines in the late 1940's.

The Pennsylvania's principal rival, the New York Central, also considered extended electrification in the immediate post-war period.

"A Practical Evaluation of Railroad Motive Power," the celebrated 1947 work on railroad motive power by Paul W. Kiefer, the Central's chief engineer, motive power and rolling stock, depicts a streamlined 5000 h.p., 2-C+C-2 electric that might have powered NYC passenger trains at speeds up to 105 m.p.h. on an expanded main line electrification. But the Central, too, decided instead in favor of dieselization.

Dieselization, of course, was a sort of self-contained form of electrification that afforded many of the advantages of electrification with far less capital investment. Like electrification, dieselization could eliminate the need to maintain the large fixed investment that was required for coaling and watering facilities for steam power, diesels substantially reduced fuel costs, and diesel motive power offered a much higher availability than steam as well.

Dieselization not only proved to be an attractive alternative to new electrification projects, but also helped bring to an end many of the early electrifications. Diesel-electric locomotives, together with improved ventilation systems, afforded a satisfactory alternative to electric power for tunnel smoke abatement, and also eliminated the need for time-consuming and expensive motive power changes at each end of an electrified zone. Thus, in scarcely more than a decade after the end of World War II dieselization had brought electric operation to an end in the Boston & Maine's Hoosac Tunnel, the B&O's Baltimore tunnel operation, the Michigan Central's Detroit River Tunnel, Great Northern's Cascade Tunnel, and the Canadian National's St. Clair Tunnel. For similar reasons, the Cleveland Union Terminal's smoke abatement electrification was shut down in 1953.

Faced with major renewal costs for aging electrification fixed plant installations and motive power, several of the roads that had electrified for reasons of general economy and efficiency of operation elected instead to de-electrify and convert to full diesel operation. The Butte, Anaconda & Pacific ended electric operation in 1967 in favor of diesels. The Milwaukee Road dieselized the Washington segment of its long electrification in 1972, while the Rocky Mountain segment in Montana and Idaho was shut down two years later. The Mexican Railway's high-voltage D.C. system, by then part of the National Railway of Mexico, was also dieselized in 1974.

The Norfolk & Western's West Virginia mountain electrification may have been the only one to be replaced by steam operation. After a major line relocation and a new tunnel were completed on N&W's Elkhorn grade in 1950, electric operation was discontinued in favor of modern steam power. The second Pocohontas region electrification came to an end under unique circumstances as well. Following merger of the Virginian and N&W in 1959, traffic was routed to take advantage of the most favorable grades on either of the two main lines. This left the former Virginian electrification with a largely one-way traffic flow that precluded effective electric motive power utilization, and the catenary came down in 1962.

There was other electrification retrenchment, too, in the several decades following the war. With much of Pennsylvania-Reading Seashore Line's commuter traffic already lost to automobiles, a requirement of the New Jersey Public Utilities Commission that all of its wooden M.U. cars be replaced by steel equipment brought an end to electric operation on the former West Jersey & Seashore in 1949. At New York City several minor branches of the New York Central's electrification were de-electrified, while diesels replaced electric power on the road's West Side freight line. At Philadelphia, a few minor sections of the PRR's extensive suburban electrification were closed.

Even as U.S. electrification retrenched, there were continued advances in electrification technology that made new electric traction installations more attractive than ever. The rapid post-war advance of the diesel-electric locomotive had brought with it the development of rugged, efficient, mass produced traction motors, trucks, drive systems, controls, and other components that would prove equally applicable to straight electric motive power. In the early 1960's the development of a new generation of silicon diode rectifiers provided a locomotive power conversion source that was cooler, more rugged, and less costly to maintain than the earlier liquid-cooled ignitron rectifiers. The last few units completed under the Pennsylvania's order for 66 E44 rectifier locomotives were fitted with the new silicon rectifiers, a change that permitted an increase in their rated capacity from 4400 h.p. to 5000 h.p., and the entire fleet was subsequently refitted.

Elsewhere in the world, the new rectifier-based, industrial frequency technology had contributed to an enormous growth in electrification, while U.S. electrified mileage had continued to decline. By the early 1970's the U.S., which had once led the world in electric operation, had declined to 17th place behind even Czechoslovakia, Austria, Norway, and Brazil. The Soviet Union, which now led the world with almost 22,500 electrified route miles, had almost 20 times the U.S. electric mileage.

If there were no new main line electrifications in North America, there were two modest projects in the 1960's which demonstrated the new electrification technology. In 1965, the Iron Ore Company of Canada completed a 6-mile automated industrial frequency electrification of an ore line in Labrador. Motive power was a fleet of five all-electric versions of a standard General Motors switcher fitted with motor-generator sets for A.C. to D.C. power conversion. A much more important project was the Muskingum Electric Railroad, a 15-mile coal railroad opened in 1968 in southeastern Ohio. Developed by the American Electric Power Company as a test-bed for the new technology of high-voltage, commercial frequency electrification, the Muskingum was electrified with a 25,000 volt, 60-cycle, single-phase A.C. system. Two E50 locomotives supplied by GE for the line were a further development of the road switcher freight locomotives built previously for the Virginian and the Pennsylvania. D.C. power for the 5000 h.p. E50's six D.C. series traction motors was supplied through a group of silicon-controlled rectifier (thyristor) diodes.

By the beginning of the 1970's, if little was actually happening in the way of major North American electrification, there was at least a steadily growing interest in its possibilities. In 1970 the Edison Electric Institute, a utility industry association, completed a detailed electrification study of the New York Central's main line between Harmon, N.Y., and Cleveland as a basis for evaluating the technical and economic feasibility of electrification of high-traffic-density railroad operations. There were about 22,000 track-miles of U.S. railroads, reported the Institute, on which traffic density warranted electrification.

Another important report, developed by a Government-Industry Task Force on Railroad Electrification, was issued by the

Federal Railroad Administration early in 1974. "Railroad electrification," reported the Task Force, "is the only available alternative to diesel-electric operations on high-density, long-haul railroad lines," and it "offers the only feasible means to utilize coal or nuclear power for intercity movements of general freight and passengers."

Through the end of the 1960's the emerging world standard for new industrial frequency electrification had been the 25,000 volt, 50- or 60-cycle, single phase A.C. system. But a new coal hauling railroad that began operating in Arizona late in 1973 established a new standard that promised ever greater economies for long-haul main line electrification. This was the Black Mesa & Lake Powell Railroad, which employed a 50,000 volt, 60-cycle, single-phase system. The higher voltage permitted the 78-mile railroad to operate from a single substation at the Navajo Generating Station at one end of the line. Three E60C box-cab, thyristor rectifier units were built for the line by GE's Erie, Pennsylvania, plant.

By the early 1970's, there was a higher level of interest in main line electrification than at any time since the beginning of the Great Depression. In 1970 the Southern Pacific completed a joint feasibility study with Southern California Edison that recommended a 760-mile, 50,000 volt electrification between El Paso and Colton, California, on the high density Sunset Route. At about the same time the Canadian Pacific began electrification studies for some 850 miles of line in the Canadian Rockies between Calgary, Alberta, and Vancouver, and on the secondary line between Golden and Sparwood, B.C., which transported a heavy—and growing—export coal traffic. The CP studies extended even to tests in Norway with a Swedish-built thyristor locomotive, and the installation of a test section of catenary in the Rockies. Burlington Northern in 1973 began studies of electrification of as much as 1200 miles of coal line in Montana, Nebraska, and Wyoming with a 50,000 volt system that was projected to reduce energy costs by as much as a third. Union Pacific, too, studied 50,000 volt electrification over some 2250 track-miles on the routes from North Platte, Nebraska, to Salt Lake City, Utah and Pocatello, Idaho. Catenary test sections were installed at two locations to study weather, maintenance, and interference problems.

In the South, Illinois Central Gulf conducted feasibility studies and an economic analysis for 50,000 volt electrification of its Chicago-New Orleans main line and some of its principal branches. The Southern Railway, jointly with General Electric, the Tennessee Valley Authority, and local power companies, initiated studies for almost 500 miles of main line electrification over its heavily trafficked Cincinnati-Chattanooga-Atlanta main line.

In the east, before its 1970 bankruptcy, the Penn Central had begun studies of electrification of its heavy freight line operating on the west bank of the Hudson River between Newark and Selkirk Yard, near Albany.

At least nine other railroads, including the Bessemer & Lake Erie, Missouri Pacific, Canadian National, Rio Grande, Santa Fe, Quebec, North Shore & Labrador, C&O/B&O, Missabe, and Katy, at least considered electrification projects.

For some of the main line railroads that considered it, electrification just wasn't economically feasible. But for most of them, electrification studies projected significant savings in operating and maintenance costs, and impressive gains in operating efficiencies, compared to diesel-electric motive power. Yet, troubled by uncertainties surrounding the long range relationship between electric power and oil fuel costs, as well as the great difficulty any of them would have in financing the enormous capital costs of electrification, none of the principal main line railroads went ahead with electrification.

Contributing, too, to a reluctance to electrify was the "moving target" presented by electrification's principal motive power rival, the diesel-electric locomotive, as each new generation of diesel power showed continuing gains in operating efficiency, reliability, and availability. In just 15 years from 1969 to 1984, for example, the energy efficiency of diesel electric power, measured in ton-miles per gallon of fuel, increased by well over a third.

While main line railroads held back on new electrifications, there were some important developments, and some modest growth, on the existing electrifications. Even before the Pennsylvania-New York Central-New Haven merger into the Penn Central in 1968-69, the Pennsylvania had begun the development of its Metroliner high speed train program for the New York-Washington corridor. Powered by four 300 h.p. traction motors on each car, and equipped with such features as solid-state acceleration, deceleration, and speed controls, the Metroliner rectifier M.U. cars were designed to attain a maximum speed of 160 m.p.h. The Pennsylvania ordered 50 of the stainless steel cars from the Budd Company, while another 11 identical cars were ordered by the Southeastern Pennsylvania Transportation Authority (SEPTA) for a State of Pennsylvania-supported service between Philadelphia and Harrisburg.

Plagued by electrical and mechanical problems, the Metroliners were two years late when they finally appeared on Penn Central timetables in 1969, and they never did prove capable of meeting all of their original speed and performance objectives. But the trains did set a new standard for high speed performance, cutting as much as 50 minutes from the best schedule ever operated by a GG1 with a 2 hour 30 minute non-stop New York-Washington timing, and they helped to reverse a downward trend in passenger traffic in the corridor.

Modest improvements initiated by the PRR to support high speed service in the New York-Washington corridor ultimately grew into the massive, federally-funded Northeast Corridor Improvement Program, which rebuilt fixed plant all the way from Washington to Boston by the time the $2.5 billion program was substantially complete by the mid-1980's. Track reconstruction, highway grade separations, electrification improvements, and new train control and signalling systems allowed Amtrak, which had acquired ownership of the Corridor in 1976, to operate at a 120 m.p.h. maximum speed.

Disappointed in the inherited Metroliner program, Amtrak returned to a more conventional locomotive-hauled approach for a new generation of high speed passenger trains for the Corridor. In 1972 the passenger carrier ordered 26 General Electric E60CP units that were a 6000 h.p., 120 m.p.h. passenger version of the units supplied to the Black Mesa & Lake Powell.

While the E60CP had originally been contemplated as the eventual replacement for Amtrak's aging GG1 fleet, tracking problems at high-speed led to trials with two European electrics and quite a different outcome. In July 1976, Amtrak put a leased Swedish State Railways 6000 h.p. ASEA Rc4 unit in trial Northeast Corridor service. Early the following year a leased French National Railways 7725 h.p. Alsthom-Atlantique unit joined the Swedish-built unit in the Corridor. The French-built locomotive was sent home after only 90 days of test operation, but the little Swedish B-B unit proved a solid success. By the end of 1977 Amtrak had placed an order for the first eight units of an AEM7 fleet that reached a total of 47 locomotives by 1982. Built by GM's Electro-Motive Division under a license from ASEA, the AEM7 was a 5800 h.p., 125 m.p.h. U.S. version of the lightweight, high-speed four-axle thyristor locomotives that ASEA had been supplying by the hundreds to the Swedish State Railways and other European systems since 1965. Late in 1987, Amtrak placed an order with Electro-Motive for another seven of the AEM7's, two of them to replace units destroyed in a wreck of the *Colonial* at Chase, Maryland, early in the year.

The speedy AEM7 proved popular for commuter services as well. In 1986 the Maryland Rail Commuter Service took delivery of four AEM7's for push-pull commuter services in Amtrak's Northeast Corridor main line between Baltimore and Washington. A year later Electro-Motive delivered another seven AEM7 units to the Southeastern Pennsylvania Transportation Authority (SEPTA) for similar push-pull commuter services on former Pennsylvania and Reading lines.

Both the Pennsylvania GG1's and the General Electric E60CP's that were originally expected to replace them were eclipsed in Amtrak's high speed Northeast Corridor service by the speedy Swedish imports. The GG1's themselves made their last runs in Amtrak service in 1980, while the E60CP's, held to a 90 m.p.h. maximum speed, were limited to service on heavy through trains in the Corridor. A substantial part of the E60CP fleet went on to new owners. Two went west in 1982 to take up coal-hauling duties on New Mexico's Navajo Mine Railroad, while another ten were sold to New Jersey Transit in 1983 for North Jersey Coast Line commuter service, where they displaced the very last survivors of a Pennsy GG1 fleet that had once numbered 139 locomotives.

GM's Electro-Motive Division, which had moved into the electrification field with the establishment of its licensing agreement with Sweden's ASEA in 1972, put two prototype freight electrics in test operation on Penn Central's former PRR electrification in 1975 and 1976. One was a 6000 h.p. C-C road switcher unit that employed EMD's standard diesel-electric trucks and traction motors, while the second was a 10,000 h.p. unit employing ASEA trucks and traction motors in a B-B-B wheel arrangement. But Penn Central electrification failed to grow, and by the early 1980's blue-clad diesels of PC successor Conrail, instead of a new generation of straight electrics, had moved in under the former Pennsy catenary.

The same movement towards public support and public ownership that provided resources for rehabilitation and expansion of urban rail transit systems during the 1960's and 1970's helped, too, to carry out modernization and modest expansion of the electrified commuter rail services at New York, Philadelphia, and Chicago.

The first commuter railroad to move towards public support was the Long Island Rail Road, which—with an annual traffic that had reached some 76 million annual passengers by 1985—ranked as America's busiest commuter railroad. Early in the 1950's the Pennsy-owned LIRR had fallen into bankruptcy and a state of near collapse. By mid-decade a publicly-supported Railroad Redevelopment Corporation had provided a basis for financing LIRR improvements, which added 140 new M.U. cars to another 80 earlier post-war electrics that helped to carry the traffic in the third rail territory that handled the majority of LIRR commuters. In 1986 the Long Island became the first major publicly-owned railroad when it was purchased from the PRR by the State of New York and became part of the regional Metropolitan Transportation Authority. Massive improvements financed by the MTA over the next several years added 770 Budd M-1 Metropolitan M.U. cars to the LIRR fleet between 1968 and 1972, permitting the retirement of hundreds of aged LIRR M.U. cars, some of which went as far back as 1908. Easily the most advanced commuter electrics ever built at the time of their delivery, the stainless steel cars were fitted with four 150 h.p. traction motors that gave the M-1 a 100 m.p.h. maximum speed potential and a 2.1 m.p.h. per second maximum acceleration rate. A later order went to General Electric for another 152 M-1 cars, and during 1985-86 Budd successor Transit America supplied 174 M-3 M.U. cars that represented a second generation of high performance M.U. cars for the Long Island.

Modernization of the LIRR also brought substantial expansion of the railroad's electrified territory. By 1970 new third rail had been energized over the LIRR Main Line between Mineola and Hicksville, and on the Port Jefferson Branch from Hicksville to Huntington. And by the end of 1987 the Long Island had completed an additional electrification project that further extended third rail operation over another 23 miles of the railroad's Main Line, from Hicksville to Ronkonkoma.

Similar modernization programs were carried out for the former New York Central and New Haven commuter lines north of the New York City, which successively passed through Penn Central and Conrail ownership before becoming—in 1983—the Metropolitan Transportation Authority's publicly-owned Metro-North Commuter Railroad.

Early post-war equipment modernization for the two systems had included a hundred new third rail M.U. cars supplied to the New York Central by St. Louis Car in 1949-50, and a hundred ignitron rectifier M.U. cars for the New Haven that were built by Pullman-Standard in 1954. Pullman-Standard built another 87 New York State-financed M.U.'s for the New York Central in the early 1960's. Aside from this equipment, both lines continued to operate through the early 1970's with their original rolling stock. New York's MTA acquired 128 GE-Budd high performance third rail M-1 M.U. cars for the former NYC lines in 1972 that were essentially identical to the Long Island's M-1 cars, while the following year MTA and the Connecticut Department of Transportation jointly financed a fleet of 144 similar General Electric M-2 Cosmopolitan high performance rectifier M.U. cars that were equipped for A.C. operation on the former New Haven lines. Subsequent orders increased the Metro-North M-1 and M-2 fleet to more than 400 cars. During 1983-84 Metro-North received 130 Budd M-3-a third rail M.U. cars that were essentially identical to the 174 M-3's supplied to the Long Island. With its commuter traffic building steadily, Metro-North began receiving a new fleet of 54 M-4 M.U. cars for its former New Haven A.C. lines into Connecticut late in 1987. Built by Japan's Tokyu Car Corporation, the M-4's were designed for operation in a semi-permanently coupled motor-trailer-motor "triplex" arrangement instead of the married-pair configuration of previous Long Island and Metro-North M.U. cars.

Metro-North, too, expanded its electrified territory, with a 28-mile extension of Harlem Division third rail north from North White Plains to Brewster that opened in 1984.

Across the Hudson River from New York City, public support of commuter services was provided through the New Jersey Department of Transportation beginning in 1968. By 1983 ownership of electrified commuter services on the former Lackawanna and New York & Long Branch railroads had passed to the State-owned New Jersey Transit Rail Operations, which also operated high speed commuter services in Amtrak's Northeast Corridor main line.

The first New Jersey investment in commuter rail was a fleet of 35 stainless steel Jersey Arrow I M.U. cars built by St. Louis Car Company in 1968. Capable of a 100 m.p.h. maximum speed, the Jersey Arrows permitted Penn Central to offer the world's fastest commuter service between New York and Trenton. Subsequent Arrow II and Arrow III orders from General Electric and other builders eventually replaced all older rolling stock in former PRR commuter services.

A major NJ Transit modernization project was completed in 1984, when the former Lackawanna's Morris & Essex Division electrified suburban routes were converted from their original 3000 volt D.C. power supply to a modern commercial frequency 25,000 volt, 60-cycle, single phase A.C. system. At the same time, the line's original M.U. rolling stock was replaced by a fleet of 140 Jersey Arrow III stainless steel M.U. cars.

On its North Jersey Coast Line, the former New York & Long Branch Railroad, NJ Transit extended electrfication some 5 miles from South Amboy to Matawan in 1982 while work started in 1985 on a further 16 miles of catenary that would extend beyond Matawan to Long Branch.

At Philadelphia, public support of electric commuter services on the Pennsylvania and Reading railroads began in 1958 with Operation Northwest, a city-supported subsidy program for commuter services on the two lines. This was followed by creation of the regional Southeastern Pennsylvania Transportation Authority (SEPTA) in 1963. After first acquiring the local transit lines in the Philadelphia area, SEPTA became the owner of the former PRR and Reading commuter services in 1983.

New equipment for the two railroads was first provided in 1963, when the City of Philadelphia purchased 55 new 85 m.p.h. Budd Silverliner M.U.'s that were similar to the six prototype rectifier cars developed for the Pennsylvania in 1958. Additional modern cars were added to the Reading M.U. fleet in 1974, when General Electric delivered 14 State of New Jersey-financed cars for the railroad's New Jersey services. Subsequent Silverliner orders built by St. Louis Car Company and GE eventually increased the SEPTA M.U. fleet to some 343 cars.

Several extensions to the Philadelphia electrified commuter network were completed during the post war years. The Reading completed two modest extensions to its electric territory in 1966 and 1974, when the A.C. catenary was extended 5 miles on the Newtown Branch to Fox Chase and 2 miles to Warminster on the Hatboro line. Two much more amibitious projects were completed by SEPTA in 1984. One of these was a 2-mile subway under downtown Philadelphia that linked Reading Terminal and the former PRR Suburban Station, permitting SEPTA to consolidate the separate PRR and Reading commuter lines into a single system. A second project provided SEPTA with a new line into the Philadelphia International Airport, permitting a new high speed service to the airport terminal area from SEPTA's commuter railroad system.

At Chicago, the Illinois Central began a modernization of its electrified commuter service in 1971, when the St. Louis Car Company began the delivery of a fleet of 130 new double-deck M.U. cars capable of a 75 m.p.h. maximum speed. Another 36 identical cars, built by Canada's Bombardier in 1978, permitted IC to complete the replacement of its original 1920's M.U. car fleet.

Just like the eastern commuter lines, IC's Chicago service made the transition from railroad to public ownership. New cars for the IC service were initially acquired by the Chicago South Suburban Mass Transit District, and in 1987 Metra, the commuter rail subsidiary of the Chicago's area's Regional Transportation Authority, took title to the commuter railroad itself.

Another modest example of the new industrial frequency electrification technology went on line in 1976, when the Texas Utilities Generating Company began operating a 19-mile coal line serving the company's Monticello Generating Plant near Mount Pleasant, Texas. A second, 13-mile Texas Utilities line began operating at the company's Martin Lake generating station the following year. Both lines were equipped with a 25,000 volt, 60 cycle, single-phase A.C. power supply. Seven E25B 2500 h.p. thyristor, rectifier locomotives were supplied for the two lines by General Electric's Erie, Pennsylvania, works.

Two more new electrifications, both employing the 50,000 volt, 60 cycle A.C. system, opened in western North America early in 1984. The Deseret Western Railway, a 35-mile coal line, began operating between the Deserado Mine in northwestern Colorado and the Bonanza Power Plant across the Utah state line to the west. Two 6000 h.p. General Electric E60 units supplied the motive power.

In Western Canada the British Columbia Railway energized the catenary on a 50,000 volt A.C. electrification of its 80-mile Tumbler Ridge branch that was seen as a prototype for a much wider Canadian electrification. Seven 6000 h.p., thyristor controlled locomotives hauled a heavy coal traffic out of Rocky Mountain mines on its way to the Pacific Ocean through the port at Prince Rupert. General Motors of Canada built the GF6C locomotives, which employed ASEA technology through GM's licensing arrangement with the Swedish manufacturer.

Encouraged by the success of the Tumbler Ridge line, British Columbia Railway was studying an extension of its new electrification over another 70 miles from Anzac to Prince George.

In Central America there was considerably more electrification activity.

Early in 1982 the Ferrocarriles de Costa Rica energized the catenary on some 66 miles of 3-foot, 6-inch gauge line along the Atlantic coast of Costa Rica newly electrified with a 25,000 volt, 60-cycle, single phase A.C. system. A dozen dual-voltage 1600 h.p. locomotives supplied by France's Alsthom were capable of operation on both the new electrification and the earlier 15,000 volt, 20-cycle installation on Costa Rica's west coast.

In Mexico, the National Railways began work on what promised to be the first major new main line electrification in North America since the Pennsylvania's great eastern lines program of the 1930's. First priority for NdeM electrification was the 200-mile section of main line between Mexico City and Irapuato, where freight traffic was reaching the saturation point on one of the railway's heaviest routes. Construction of an entirely new double-track route between the two cities began in the late 1970's, and work on a 25,000 volt, 50-cycle A.C. electrification for the new route got underway several years later. General Electric completed a fleet of 39 of its 6000 h.p. E60C locomotives for the new system in 1983, by which time the electrification was to have been operational. With completion of both the new line and the electrification delayed by Mexico's economic crisis of the early 1980's, the big GE electrics have been sitting idle at Salinas de Hidalgo ever since their completion. By late 1988, however, the catenary was scheduled to be energized over the first 136 miles of the new route between Mexico City and Queretaro. Completion of the balance of the new line will follow. Next, NdeM will extend its 25,000 volt catenary north over the main line to San Luis Potosi. Eventually, NdeM plans to have its entire core system, which accounts for some 80 percent of its traffic, under electric operation.

While both Canada and Mexico had at least made a modest beginning to new main line electrification with the B.C. Railway and NdeM projects, U.S. railroads still seemed to be waiting for someone else to be the first with an extensive trunk line electrification. When, or even if, major electrification was ever going to happen in the U.S. was just as uncertain in 1988 as it had been for the previous two or three decades. Yet the arguments for a shift to electric traction seemed to grow stronger every year.

The ability to draw power from the commercial power grid that rectifier technology made possible, combined with the development of lightweight, economical catenary systems, promised to reduce the potential high cost of electrification; some studies suggested that costs could be brought down to the range of $80,000 to $100,000 per mile. The cost of straight electric motive power was projected at anywhere from 50 to 80 percent of that for diesel power of equivalent horsepower, although electrics would cost anywhere from 50 to 70 percent more on the basis of equivalent tractive effort. Quantity production, however, promised to bring the cost for an equivalent tractive effort rating down to a comparable level. On a per-ton-mile basis electric locomotive maintenance costs promised to be well below half those for diesels, and electric power offered a substantially higher availability than diesel power.

Relative fuel costs remained one of the big unknowns in any electric-versus-diesel comparison. But while oil prices had dropped back substantially after the enormous increases of the 1970's, most long-range analyses suggested that much higher oil prices were probable. One 1986 report, for example, predicted that $30 per barrel oil (in 1985 dollars) would be back by 1995. With its ability to draw upon alternate energy sources through central electric generating plants, railroad electrification promised at least a relative energy cost stability.

Contributing, too, to an increasingly favorable outlook for economic electrification were several important trends in American railroading. Long term traffic growth, together with a substantial concentration of traffic through mergers and elimination of redundant routes, combined to increase the railroad mileage on which tonnage levels made electrification economically feasible. In 1987, for example, U.S. freight traffic of some 941 billion ton-miles represented an all-time record, and was close to 15 percent above the level of a decade earlier.

A growing market for piggyback, container, and other fast freight services had also created a demand for high horsepower, high-speed motive power that electrification was uniquely well-equipped to provide. Still another market for electrification was represented by a growing interest in the development of very high speed passenger services, for which electric operation was exceptionally well suited.

As always, the enormous capital investment required for significant electrification remained a formidable barrier. But the railroad that first found a way to do it promised to gain extraordinary advantages over its competitors in the efficiency, economy, and quality of service that it could provide with electric power. When—and if—that happens it should set in motion a long-delayed shift to electrification of principal rail routes in North America, and the promise of main line electrification, so long denied, may be achieved at last.

Early in the twentieth century, the need for electrification in Philadelphia was compelling. Congestion at the Broad Street Station and the pall of coal smoke from the steam engines created both operating and community relations problems. Not one to experiment too much, management of the Pennsylvania Railroad approached electrification carefully. It even took the then extraordinary step of hiring a consultant, George Gibbs, who by 1913 had formed the firm of Gibbs and Hill, a firm that in 1988 still serves the railroad industry. The Pennsylvania Railroad had used direct current, but direct current was more adaptable to terminal-type operations. The Paoli service was converted to electrification using alternating current on September 11, 1915. The Chestnut Hill service was converted in April, 1918. The lines to West Chester, Pennsylvania, and Wilmington, Delaware, were converted in 1928, followed by electrification to Trenton, New Jersey, in 1930. In 1976, Conrail was created from the ruins of Penn Central and the Reading Railroad. The commuter services of these two railroads were combined under Conrail's administration. In 1988, all commuter service in Philadelphia is operated directly by the Southeastern Pennsylvania Transportation Authority (SEPTA). ABOVE: From 1915 to the 1970's, commuter service was provided by the venerable MP54's in Philadelphia. In true

Pennsylvania Railroad fashion, the MP54's were home-designed, home-built cars adapted from a design used for locomotive-hauled trains. Electrical equipment was provided by Westinghouse, a significant on-line customer. In its twilight years, an eight-car train of MP54's in pure Tuscan Red with gold lettering was rounding the curve between Radnor and St. David's on the Paoli line on August 10, 1967. *(John J. Bowman photo)* LEFT: The sea of Tuscan Red was broken in 1958 by six stainless steel cars from Budd Co. They were appropriately named "Pioneer III" cars by their builders. In 1958, these cars saw service in the heart of the rush hour on the "Paoli skip-stop." When a young railfan sought them out, he was looked upon with disdain by the gatemen at Suburban Station, who referred to these cars as "tin cans." Car 150, the "series car," led this train at Villanova in 1958. Five of the six cars exist in 1988. *(Bruce C. Bente photo)* Across downtown, at Reading Terminal, cars built by Bethlehem Steel began providing electrified service on July 26, 1931, to suburban communities north and east of Philadelphia. ABOVE: In its traditional livery of Pullman Green, a four-car train was south of Jenkintown on April 13, 1964. In 1988, three train sets of these cars still operate in regular SEPTA commuter service. TOP RIGHT: Reading Railroad also purchased a group of the "Pioneer III" cars. This train was at Jenkintown on April 13, 1964. *(Two photos WDM)* BOTTOM LEFT: The "Pioneer III" cars were the predecessors of the "Silverliners," which were delivered primarily between 1973 and 1977 by General Electric. They were paid for with the assistance of public funds. On June 12, 1976, this Conrail-operated train was at Jenkintown. *(FWS)*

The Pennsylvania Railroad also conducted significant commuter operations in New Jersey. Electrification between Trenton and New York City was completed on January 16, 1933. ABOVE: New Jersey, as well as the Philadelphia area, was the domain of the MP54's. On May 3, 1969, this train from Trenton is departing Princeton Junction. At the right is the famed Princeton Shuttle. RIGHT: The new generation of cars began in 1968 when the Jersey Arrows were delivered by St. Louis Car Co. Crews at Sunnyside Yard had a less dignified name, "Silver Flush," because of their retention toilets which required servicing. In 1988, these cars are now in diesel-hauled, push-pull service. On May 28, 1969, Car 118 had just left the Bergen Tunnels. BELOW: Service in 1988 is provided by 300 Jersey Arrow II and Jersey Arrow III cars built by General Electric between 1974 and 1978. These trains were at Princeton Junction on October 8, 1979. *(All FWS)*

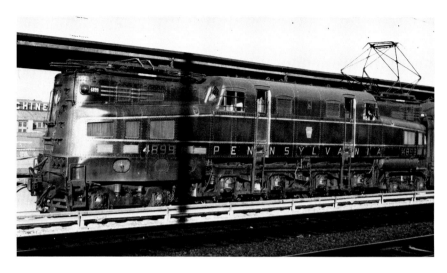

For years, the Pennsylvania Railroad experimented with motive power for both freight and passenger service. For passenger trains, it came down to two basic designs: the R1 and the GG1. ABOVE: The one and only R1 posed at Manhattan Transfer. *(Mehlenbeck Collection)* This unit was pitted in test against the original GG1, "Old Rivets." Both locomotives could reach 120 mph, but, more importantly, the GG1 was easier on the track. The GG1 was a wondrous machine. As author Middleton said in *When the Steam Roads Electrified,* "The immense proportions and flowing contours of Pennsylvania Railroad's famous Raymond Loewy-styled GG1 contributed to the drama of 'The Standard Railroad of the World.' " TOP RIGHT: A traditional view of a GG1 in its early years at Wynnewood, Pennsylvania. *(Krambles Collection)* "Old Rivets" was built in August, 1934. The first production models of the GG1's were delivered in May, 1935. Deliveries continued until June, 1943. In total, there were 139 units that served in both passenger and freight service for the Pennsylvania, Penn Central, Conrail, Amtrak and the New Jersey Department of Transportation. The first retirements came on March 3, 1966. The last runs occurred amid much ceremony on October 29, 1983. BOTTOM RIGHT: Motor 4900 was hauling a string of P70 coaches at Jericho Park, Maryland, on May 10, 1969. *(FWS)* OVERLEAF LEFT: If one stood near the mouth of the Bergen Tunnels in Secaucus, New Jersey, the approach of a train could be predicted by the rush of air being forced out of the tunnel. Within moments, the train would burst from the tunnel and sweep into the long curve and head southwest across the Jersey Meadow toward Newark at 60 mph or more. Such was the scene in 1960. *(George C. White photo, Donald Duke Collection)* In 1977, the "Friends of the GG1" funded the repainting of Motor 4935 into its historic Pennsylvania Railroad livery of Brunswick green, with Keystone and pinstripes. On October 27, 1979, in its 36th year of service, 4935 was southbound on Train 105, a Metroliner schedule, at Landover, Maryland. The last run of the 4935 was on October 10, 1981. Despite its age, Amtrak was willing to put the motor on its fastest schedules. *(WDM)*

Desire for high-speed ground transportation between Washington, D.C., and New York City led to the development of the Metroliners. The cars evolved from high-speed tests with modified Silverliners. The Metroliners were ordered in 1966 before these tests were completed. A prototype car did not precede the production order. As a result, scheduled service did not begin until January 16, 1969. Despite continual mechanical problems (a mechanic was a part of the train crew), the Metroliners did reverse the downtrend in railroad riding on the Northeast Corridor. RIGHT: Two of the 61 cars in the fleet were at their builder's (Budd Co.) plant in 1968. *(Krambles Collection)* BELOW: A six-car train led by Car 858 was about to enter the Bergen Tunnel on May 28, 1969. *(FWS)* BOTTOM RIGHT: Car 889 leads a train into Wilmington, Delaware, on January 26, 1980. *(WDM)* As the 1980's progressed, the cars were removed from service on the Northeast Corridor and renamed Capitoliners. They were assigned to the Keystone Service between Philadelphia and Harrisburg. As the mechanical problems continued, AEM-7's and then diesels started pulling the cars with pantographs raised to power auxiliaries. The Capitoliners were removed from service on January 25, 1988. Late in 1987, 10 of the cars started to appear, without motors, as cab cars in push-pull service on Amtrak's San Diegans and, in 1988, operate between San Diego, Los Angeles and Santa Barbara, California. The carbody design was used by Amtrak for its Amfleet cars which serve throughout the United States.

144

In its search to find a replacement for the GG1, Amtrak ordered 26 E-60 electric locomotives from General Electric. The first two units were delivered in December, 1974. However, problems developed with the trucks and acceptance of the locomotives was delayed for one year. Twenty of the units were equipped with headend power (HEP) and six units had steam generators. ABOVE: Locomotive 974 was at Bell Tower, Claymont, Delaware, on January 26, 1980. *(WDM)* LEFT: On October 29, 1979, Locomotive 970 was southbound at Landover, Maryland. BELOW: Shortly after acceptance of the fleet, train number 177, "Senator," was crossing the Raritan River at New Brunswick, New Jersey, on July 25, 1976. *(Two photos FWS)* Following delivery of the AEM-7's, Amtrak sold two of the E-60's to the Navajo Mine railroad in 1982 and ten of the E-60's to NJDOT in 1983, where they replaced the last survivors of the GG1's. In 1988, Amtrak rebuilt some of its remaining E-60's and renumbered all of them in the 600 series.

In 1972, General Motor's Electro-Motive Division signed licensing agreements with ASEA of Sweden to market its technology to the American railroad industry. First to appear were two freight locomotives to be tested by Penn Central and Conrail. ABOVE: GM 1975, Model GM6C, was a 6,000-horsepower, C-C wheel arrangement unit that began tests in April, 1975. This photo was taken on August 13, 1975. *(Schneider Collection)* BELOW: GM 1976, Model GM10B, was a 10,000-horsepower, B-B-B wheel arrangement. On this unit, the ASEA technology included motors, transmission and trucks. GM 1976 entered

service about September 9, 1976. On September 23, 1976, it was at Middleton, Pennsylvania. By March, 1979, both units were returned to EMD. No sales resulted as Conrail shut down its electric freight operations about this time. *(E. A. Lewis photo)* The outlook for passenger motors was much brighter. Amtrak leased two electric locomotives, one from Sweden and the other from France, for test purposes. Amtrak X996, nee French National Railways CC-21003, was leased from Alsthom-Atlantique for a six-month period. The 7,725-horsepower unit, which came ashore at Port Elizabeth, New Jersey, on January 24, 1977, was sent home after days. 90 days. Amtrak X995 was an ASEA Rc4, which was fabricated in Falun, Sweden, in June, 1976. By October, this 6,000-horsepower locomotive was in test service on the Northeast Corridor. The test results were impressive. Amtrak ordered 47 units of Model Rc4a. The model number became AEM-7 and consisted of ASEA technology in a Budd carbody assembled by EMD. The first test run of the prototype unit, Amtrak 900, was on January 23, 1980, five days after Amtrak received delivery. ABOVE: The 900 was northbound with its test train at Wilmington, Delaware, on January 26, 1980. *(WDM)* The 900 was the unit behind the 903 on January 4, 1987, and they both were destroyed in the tragic accident of the *Colonial* at Chase, Maryland. ABOVE: On April 1, 1983, the 934 was at BWI station. *(FWS)* BOTTOM RIGHT: The 927 passed through Lanham, Maryland, on October 23, 1981. BOTTOM LEFT: EMD found other buyers for the AEM-7. In 1986, the Maryland Rail Commuter Service took delivery of four AEM-7's. *(Alex Mayes photo)* On March 12, 1987, MARC 4901 was on a Baltimore-Washington commuter train at BWI Airport. Because of the similarity in road numbers to the GG1, crews refer to these units as GG2's. On November 13, 1987, EMD delivered the first of seven AEM-7's to SEPTA for use in push-pull commuter service in Philadelphia. In October, 1988, Amtrak began receiving nine more AEM-7's. In 1988, a fourth customer appeared: New Jersey Transit ordered six units for 1990 delivery. Finally there was a successful replacement for the GG1.

When the Pennsylvania Railroad completed the Philadelphia-Paoli electrification in 1915, there was no question the AC electrification would be extended westward, perhaps as far as Pittsburgh. Particular attention was paid to the mountain crossing west of Altoona, but electrics grinding around Horseshoe Curve were not to be. In any event, a durable freight locomotive was needed. In August, 1917, the first experimental locomotive, "Big Liz," appeared. She was followed by three Class L5's in 1924. Twenty more L5's were built. Attention then turned to passenger locomotives. The P5 was introduced for heavy passenger work. In addition to the two prototypes between 1932 and 1935, 90 more of the P5's were built by General Electric, Baldwin-Westinghouse and its own Altoona shops. The P5's developed problems in the high-speed heavy passenger service, so the Pennsylvania's search continued for a high-speed passenger locomotive. The GG1 filled that need and the P5's settled into freight duties where they did yeoman work until the 1950's. ABOVE: P5a, 4726 and 4734, each 3,750-horsepower locomotives, were westbound at Dale entering the freight route between Philadelphia and Thorndale on December 18, 1956. *(John J. Bowman photo)* LEFT: Motor 4714 was at Smith on the Susquehanna Branch in September, 1958. *(FWS)* The Susquehanna Branch, or more properly the Atglen and Susquehanna Branch, the so-called Low Grade Line, begins in Enola Yard and follows the west side of the Susquehanna River to a point opposite Columbia, Pennsylvania. There it crosses the river and passes south of Lancaster,

rejoining the main line at Parkesburg. Together with the Trenton Cutoff from east of Parkesburg to Morrisville, Pennsylvania, freight trains could be moved free of the mainline and could avoid the congestion in Philadelphia. The Low Grade Line, together with the Columbia and Port Deposit Branch (the "Port Road"), was electrified together with the mainline to Harrisburg on January 15, 1938. ABOVE: GG1 4822 was on an eastbound freight on the Low Grade Line crossing Conestoga Creek at Safe Harbor, Pennsylvania, in 1962. Below this train a freight can be seen on the "Port Road." The "Port Road" connects the Low Grade Line at Columbia with the Washington-Philadelphia line at Perrysville, Maryland. The GG1's were equally at home with freight as well as passenger service. Motor 4869 was on the "Port Road" one mile south of Drumore, Pennsylvania, on May 30, 1969. *(Two photos FWS)*

In 1951, the Pennsylvania Railroad sought replacements for the P5. Again, prototype locomotives were ordered. ABOVE: General Electric built three two-unit locomotives, Class E2b, using the same type of motors as in the P5 and GG1 motors. The two units combined produced 5,000 horsepower. Motor 4941 was at General Electric on June 11, 1951. *(Krambles Collection)* TOP RIGHT: Westinghouse provided two two-unit locomotives which introduced new technology to the railroad. These 6,000-horsepower units, Class E36, with a B-B-B wheel arrangement, were equipped with ignitron rectifiers to provide DC power to the traction motors. On May 19, 1956, 4996 led a southbound freight train past Bellevue Tower near Wilmington, Delaware. BELOW: What emerged from these tests were the 4,400-horsepower, Class E-44, locomotives built by General Electric between 1960 and 1963. These 66 locomotives were essentially an upgraded version of the Virginian Railroad rectifier locomotives built by General Electric in late 1956 and early 1957. BELOW: Unit 4417 was at Columbia, Pennsylvania, in 1962. The ignitron rectifiers presented some problems and technology had advanced so the 37th and the last five units were delivered with silicon rectifiers. The resulting model was designated E44a and had 5,000 continuous horsepower. Ultimately, 22 more units of the fleet were rebuilt with silicon rectifiers. BOTTOM RIGHT: Units 4433 and 4416 are

eastbound on the Atglen and Susquehanna Branch north of Columbia, Pennsylvania, along the Susquehanna River in the summer of 1970. *(Three photos FWS)* The Virginian Railway was faced with a critical need to replace its aging electric motive power to move coal in the Pocahontas region of Virginia. General Electric delivered 12 ignitron-rectifier units, Class EL-C, which delivered 3,300 horsepower. Because of their appearance, they became known as "Bricks." The Norfolk & Western acquired the Virginian, and the electrics had their last run on the Virginian on June 30, 1962. In 1963, the New York, New Haven & Hartford Railroad bought the "Bricks" for $20,000 each (about 5% of original cost for units that were six years old). They were painted brilliant red-orange with striping and black trim and put in service by the fall of 1963. LEFT: An ex-Virginian unit, now New Haven 302, was hauling freight for its new owner. *(Jonathan D. Boyer)* When the New Haven was absorbed by the Penn Central, the "Bricks" moved to New Jersey and Pennsylvania and were designated Class E33. ABOVE: Penn Central 4602 was on the "Port Road" at Fishing Creek, Pennsylvania, on September 5, 1970. *(FWS)* On November 22, 1979, Conrail terminated its electric operations. The E33 and E44 units were put in dead storage and the wires were removed from the "Low Grade" and "Port Road." Eight of the E44's found their way to NJDOT in 1983, which stored them until 1987 and then traded them to Amtrak. In 1988, the E44's are in work service on the Northeast Corridor for Amtrak. They are now numbered in the 500 series. Conrail traded the remaining units with General Electric for diesel locomotives.

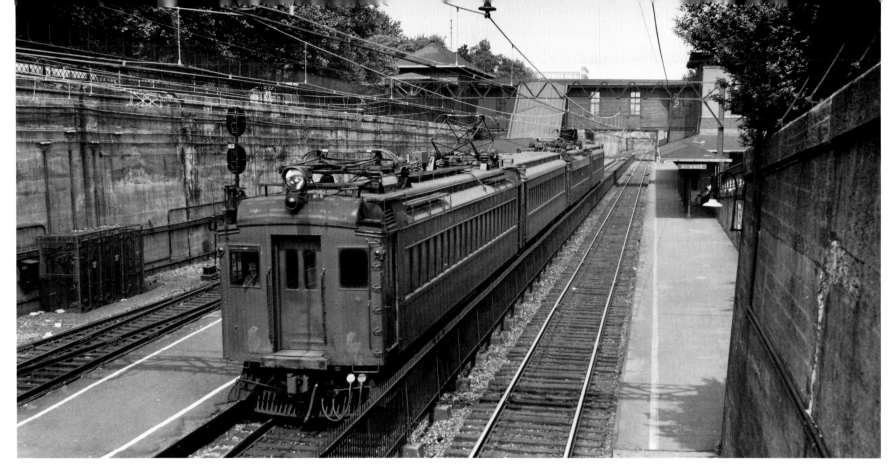

The Delaware Lackawanna & Western Railroad electrified its commuter service between 1928 and 1931. Thomas Edison opened the controller on the first trip to Montclair on September 3, 1930. By January 25, 1931, the entire service was converted when electric trains began operating to Gladstone. If there were similarities with the Illinois Central suburban electrification, that is because the DL&W hired James Thorp as Engineer of Electric Traction. Mr. Thorp came from the Illinois Central and, prior to that, from the Virginian and the New South Wales Railway in Australia. Pullman Car & Manufacturing Company built 141 motor cars of design very similar to those provided to the Illinois Central. An equal number of trailer cars were converted from steam-hauled coaches by American Car & Foundry in Berwick, Pennsylvania. ABOVE: In a scene of very traditional railroading, a train from Hoboken arrived in Summit, New Jersey, on May 28, 1969. RIGHT: On June 15, 1970, two Morristown trains pass at West End Tower at the west portal of the Bergen Tunnel. The diesel-powered trains to Boonton and ex-Erie Railroad destinations diverge here. *(Both FWS)* On August 24, 1984, these cars rolled their last miles. The 3,000-volt DC electrification was shut down. On Monday, August 27, 1984, commuters rode to work in Jersey Arrow III cars under a 25,000-volt, 60 hertz AC electrification. The reelectrification project took four years and cost $477 million.

152

Volumes could be written about the Long Island Railroad. We will take a brief look. The Long Island was chartered in 1834, and the first electrification project was completed in 1905. George Gibbs was the consulting engineer. Over the years, the railroad had more than its fair share of trials and tribulations. TOP LEFT: In 1988, commuters ride in a fleet of "Metropolitans." 770 of these cars were built by Budd Co. between 1968 and 1971, followed by 152 cars from General Electric in 1973 and 174 cars from Budd Co. in 1985. On May 22, 1970, this train was near Port Washington, New York. *(FWS)* In earlier periods, the roster was considerably more diverse. BOTTOM LEFT: Long Island's cars reflected years of Pennsylvania Railroad ownership. A train of MP54's approaches Woodside (61st Street) in Queens on the densely utilized trackage between Penn Station and Jamaica. *(WDM)* ABOVE: If it is a "double deck" car leading, it must be a Babylon train. It is! This Babylon local was at Seaford on May 22, 1970. *(FWS)* The first bi-level car entered service on August 13, 1932. Two more came in 1937; ten cars came in 1947; and, finally, a production order of 50 cars was delivered between September, 1948, and May, 1949. They spent virtually their entire careers in Babylon service. Improvements to the Long Island continue. On January 18, 1988, full electric service began over 23.5 miles between Hicksville and Ronkonkoma. The project, which started in 1983, was the biggest electrification project on the Long Island since 1925. The cost was $168 million, and the project was part of a $2.1 billion, 10-year improvement program. Average savings of 26 minutes in transit time to New York City resulted from this electrification. Also opened in 1988 was the new West Side Yard in New York City. Ahead is a rebuilding of the Jamaica complex.

Author Middleton described New Haven's electrification as a "bold venture." The New Haven was a pioneer in long-distance AC electrification. FACING PAGE TOP: Motor 0319 led this train at Port Chester, New York, on September 18, 1940. 0319 was one of 27 heavy-passenger motors delivered by Baldwin-Westinghouse between 1919 and 1928. The arrival of the last 10 units in 1928 finally removed steam engines from passenger trains into New York City. BOTTOM: General Electric achieved success in high-speed, passenger-service AC motors when it delivered the 10 units of the 0351-0360 series in 1931. The 2-C + C-2 wheel arrangement was the prototype for future New Haven passenger units as well as the Pennsylvania Railroad's GG1's. Designed to handle 15 heavyweight cars, Motor 0353 was having a relatively easy time with this train at Port Chester, New York, on September 18, 1940. *(Two photos Wallace M. Rogers, Krambles Collection)* ABOVE: When General Electric delivered the six units of the 0360, EP-4 class, in 1938, the streamline era of electric motive power began on the New Haven. Unit 360, originally 0366, was at Woodlawn Junction in June, 1954. *(Herbert H. Harwood, Jr.)* TOP RIGHT: The 10 units in the EP-5 class, road numbers 370-379, were the last electrics built for the New Haven. Delivered by General Electric in 1955, these ignitron-rectifier units had a relatively short service life. Four were out of service when Penn Central took over in 1969. On May 23, 1970, PC 4974 was at Woodlawn Junction. By early 1977, they were all out of service, and were scrapped by May, 1979. *(FWS)*

New Haven's commuter service has been praised but mostly condemned as inadequate, late and cold in winter—hot in summer, and has received a litany of other complaints. Since public ownership, the complaints have subsided but the service has a chronic problem: not enough seats for those who want to ride. Despite all this, commuters are a hearty lot who are very loyal to their trains. FACING PAGE TOP: Can you imagine boarding these open platform cars in snowy, cold weather? These open platformed cars arrived between 1909 and 1912 and served until 1955. *(Sprague Library)* BOTTOM LEFT: Between 1926 and 1931, the "roundroof" cars were delivered by Osgood Bradley. On July 21, 1970, some of the survivors of these 104 cars were still operating. These cars were crossing the Harlem River. *(FWS)* BOTTOM RIGHT: In 1954, the 100 "washboards" arrived from Pullman-Standard. These cars were equipped with ignitron rectifiers. This train was crossing the West River on the west side of New Haven. The "washboards" were removed from service in 1976. *(WDM)* ABOVE: Beginning in 1972, the M-2 series of cars was placed in service on the former New Haven lines. Known as "Cosmopolitans," this train was at Milford, Connecticut, on October 11, 1982. In 1988, service was provided by the M-2 and the M-3 cars, which were recent arrivals from Tokyo Car. RIGHT: In the early 1980's, there was a brief revival of the "washboards" on the New Canaan branch because of the chronic shortage of cars. A decade earlier, on October 11, 1970, this train was at Talmadge Hill, the first station south of New Canaan, Connecticut. *(Two photos FWS)*

The New York Central has operated commuter service on its Harlem and Hudson lines since the nineteenth century. Electrification was accomplished between 1906 and 1913. FACING PAGE TOP: On July 21, 1970, a train of the "middle era" of New York Central cars approached the 138th Street station in Bronx, New York. The last of these cars were scrapped in October, 1971. *(FWS)* BOTTOM LEFT: The "middle era" of cars was built by Standard Steel Car between 1917 and 1929. The 145 cars in this group supplemented the original fleet of 180 cars in 1906 plus 31 cars which were delivered in 1910 and 1913. This northbound train at Woodlawn, New York, in June, 1954, had one of the original cars in the train. *(Herbert H. Harwood, Jr.)* BOTTOM RIGHT: The New York Central started to replace its fleet when 100 cars were delivered in 1950 followed by 87 cars in 1962 and 1965. A train of these later cars was at Woodlawn Junction on May 23, 1970. In 1972, the MTA funded the purchase of 128 M-1 "Metropolitan" cars. Since January 1, 1983, the operations of the former New York Central lines as well as the New Haven lines have been conducted by Metro North, a subsidiary of New York's Metropolitan Transportation Authority. On April 30, 1984, Metro North completed a 29-mile electrification and rehabilitation of the Harlem line from North White Plains to Brewster North. 142 new M-3 cars were a part of this project. This was the first extension of the electrification since 1931. *(FWS)* ABOVE: New York Central's commuter operations extended beyond the traditional electrified territory. Electric locomotives were used to pull these commuter trains into Grand Central Terminal. In July, 1950, two motors were hauling this train southbound at White Plains. *(RVM)*

New York Central's "Electric Zone" reached North White Plains in March, 1910, and Croton-on-Hudson in May, 1913. FACING PAGE TOP: Among the most famous locomotives in the United States were the S class motors. Some of these units served over 60 years. Between 1904 and 1909, 47 of these units were built by ALCO-GE. They were the original motive power of the Electric Zone and handled all classes of trains. In July, 1950, Motors 135 and 141 were southbound at North White Plains on the start of a commuter run to Grand Central Terminal. *(RVM)* BOTTOM: Between 1913 and 1926, 36 of the T class motors were built by ALCO-GE. These motors replaced the S class motors on heavier trains and were also needed to handle increased traffic. In May, 1954, Motor 275 is northbound at Spuyten Duyvil passing under the Henry Hudson Bridge. RIGHT: New York Central had, at one time, a fleet of 42 tri-powered locomotives. These units could run as either straight electrics, diesels or battery locomotives. Engine 556 was at Spuyten Duyvil in the Bronx, New York, in May, 1954. The entire fleet of these tri-powered locomotives was retired by 1957. *(Two photos Herbert H. Harwood, Jr.)*

TOP LEFT: New York Central also electrified the Cleveland Union Terminal with 17 route miles of trackage from Linndale east through the terminal to Collinwood. Motive power was 22 motors of 2-C+C-2 wheel arrangement built by ALCO-GE in 1929. These units were forerunners of the New Haven's 0350 series and the Pennsylvania's GG1's. The Cleveland Union Terminal operation was electrified from 1930 to 1953. The 22 electric motors were transferred to New York, where they served for another three decades. In September, 1953, Motor 216 turned over the westbound Cleveland-St. Louis Special to Hudson 5271 at Linndale. *(Herbert H. Harwood, Jr.)* TOP RIGHT: The Detroit River Tunnel operations between Detroit, Michigan, and Windsor, Ontario, were electrified from 1910 to 1956. In June, 1953, Motors 310 and 302, two of the six R-2 class on assignment in Detroit, are leaving the tunnel in Windsor. Seven of these R-2 class motors were rebuilt by the Chicago

South Shore & South Bend into its 700-class locomotives. *(Schneider Collection)* BOTTOM: Motor 170 was one of 12 R-1 class motors built for the Detroit operation. In 1953, this train was entering Detroit's 14th Street Yard. *(Thomas J. Dworman)* THIS PAGE TOP RIGHT: Canadian National operates an electrified commuter service in Montreal. In 1988, all of this equipment is still in service. On August 5, 1986, Motors 6724 and 6722, two of the units built by English Electric in 1924 and 1926, respectively, were between Vertu and Mt. Royal stations. BOTTOM RIGHT: CN 6727, shown on June 5, 1980, is one of three steeple-cabs delivered in 1950. OVERLEAF: In 1952, CN received 6 motor and 12 trailer cars. They are the newest equipment on the line and probably the lowest performing multiple-unit cars built after World War II. On August 5, 1986, 6741 was at Deux Montagnes, Quebec, the end of the suburban service. *(Three photos WDM)*

In 1926, the Illinois Central electrified its suburban service in Chicago. During the 1920's, 140 motor and 140 trailer cars were built by Pullman and Standard Car Company. These heavyweight cars served for 50 years. TOP LEFT: On June 11, 1956, a southbound train has just left the mainline and was emerging from the tunnel under the northbound suburban tracks and passenger and freight mains to enter the South Chicago Branch. *(WDM)* TOP RIGHT: A number of crossings of Chicago Surface Lines routes were made at grade. CSL 3262

westbound on 79th Street at Exchange Avenue awaits the passage of a southbound train to South Chicago on June 13, 1951. *(Thomas H. Desnoyers)* BELOW: The first of the Highliners came in 1971. St. Louis Car built 130 cars. 36 more cars came from Bombardier in 1978 and 1979. On May 4, 1980, this southbound train was approaching 11th Place. On May 1, 1987, the commuter operation assets were sold by the Illinois Central Gulf to Metra, the commuter rail operation of Chicago's RTA. *(WDM)*

Getting through tunnels with steam engines was a major problem for the railroads. Time was needed to clear smoke and gases from the tunnels, engine exhausts shattered the tunnel linings, gases corroded signal lines and condensed steam made for bad rail conditions. Simply operating the steam locomotive was pure torture for the engine crew. It was none too pleasant for the passengers or freight crews riding in the caboose. Electrification was a much-desired solution. TOP RIGHT: Beginning on May 27, 1911, traffic moving through Hoosac Tunnel on the Boston and Maine was hauled by Baldwin Westinghouse AC electric motors. Five motors, three for freight and two for passenger service, were delivered in 1911. These units were near duplicates of experimental New Haven Motor 071. Two more motors followed in 1917. The off-center headlight was a trademark of the B&M electrics. This eight-mile electrification was discontinued in 1946. *(Lamar M. Kelley, Krambles Collection)* LEFT: The Virginian Railway had a different type of problem. It seemingly could not get enough tractive effort from steam locomotives to move coal over the Appalachian Mountains to tidewater. Following several series of Mallets, an electrification program was announced in 1923. 134 miles of line between Roanoke, Virginia, and Mullens, West Virginia, were electrified. During 1925 and 1926, ALCO-Westinghouse delivered 36 of these split-phase motors. In 1942, Motor 106 was at Princeton, West Virginia. These three-unit motors were known as squareheads. When delivered, they were the "world's most powerful locomotives" as they generated 7,125 continuous horsepower. They could handle heavier trains in less than half the time that steam locomotives could over the mountains. *(WCJ)* ABOVE: Shortly after its delivery, Motor 127 was at Rich Creek, Virginia, on July 13, 1948. Motor 127 is one of four two-unit motors delivered by General Electric in 1948. This was an intermediate step until the rectifiers arrived in 1956 and 1957 (see Page 151). Electrified service on the Virginian ended on June 30, 1962. *(Charles A. Brown)*

Electrification solved the Great Northern's operating problems in crossing the Cascade Mountains and operating through Cascade Tunnel. ABOVE: 5014 photographed on July 11, 1943, was one of eight Y-1 class units built between 1927 and 1930. When built, they were the largest single-unit, motor-generator locomotives ever built. Each unit delivered 3,300 horsepower. They were not GN's first electric locomotives as electric operations began on July 10, 1909. Ultimately, 74 route miles between Skykomish and Wenatchee, Washington, were electrified with a 6,600-volt AC system. *(WCJ)* RIGHT: In 1947, the two W-1 class locomotives were delivered by General Electric to the GN. The locomotives were 101 feet long, weighed 360 tons and had 5,000 continuous horsepower. These locomotives exceeded the horsepower of Union Pacific's 4-8-8-4 "Big Boy" locomotives and weighed about the same as Northern Pacific's "Yellowstone" class, the heaviest steam locomotive in the U. S. GN 5019 was at Skykomish, Washington. Diesels replaced the electrics in August, 1956. *(GK)*

167

FACING PAGE: On May 24, 1961, Butte, Anaconda & Pacific 53 and 59 ease one of several daily trains down the steep grade off Butte Hill toward Rocker Yard, where it will be consolidated with other mine cuts for the trip to Anaconda, Montana. Butte's butte is in the center of the skyline. BA&P's trolley wires carried power at 2,400 volts DC, making BA&P a showplace for high-voltage DC traction. BA&P's electric locomotives were built by General Electric of mechanical design similar to units built for the Great Northern, New York Central's Detroit River Tunnel and Baltimore & Ohio electric operations. The BA&P was electrified from June, 1914, to 1967. Diesel operations continue in 1988 as the Rarus Railroad. *(Philip C. Johnson photo)* ABOVE: Late in the 1960's, American Electric Power Company decided to test the latest concepts in high-voltage, commercial frequency electricity. In 1968, it opened the 15-mile Muskingum Electric Railroad, which was electrified with a 25,000-volt, 60 hertz single-phase AC system. Two E-50 type locomotives were constructed by General Electric which evolved from the rectifiers built for the New Haven, Pennsylvania and Virginian. The 78-mile Black Mesa & Lake Powell Railroad opened in late 1973 connecting the Black Mesa mine with the Navajo Generating Station near Page, Arizona. This is the first 50,000-volt, 60 hertz single-phase system in the world. On October 12, 1983, locomotives 6004, 6003 and 6002 hauled a westbound train north of Tonalca, Arizona. *(FWS)*

When completed, The Milwaukee Road electrification covered 647 route miles from Harlowton, Montana, to Avery, Idaho, and from Othello, Washington, to Seattle and Tacoma. RIGHT: In the State of Washington, passenger trains were hauled by the five Bipolar motors built by General Electric. In a historic view, 10251 was descending Snoqualmie Pass on the west side of the Cascades. *(FWS Collection)* BELOW: E-2 was at Seattle during World War II. Note the blackout shroud on the headlight. *(WCJ)* FACING PAGE: Milwaukee Road train 17, The Columbian, is led by Westinghouse-built E-14 as it crossed the Missouri River at Lombard, Montana, on April 17, 1952. This location was near the east end of Sixteen Mile Canyon. The Columbian never was fully streamlined, as can be noted by the swayback baggage car and heavyweight car on the end. The Northern Pacific tracks can be seen under the bridge on the opposite shore of the Missouri River. *(Philip C. Johnson)*

Montana's Big Sky Country combined with the Bitterroot Mountains created some memorable scenes of The Milwaukee Road's electrification. FACING PAGE: Extra E-38 East stretched through Nine Mile Curve approximately seven miles east of Alberton, Montana, on September 10, 1950. The caboose was on the north siding switch to Soudam, Montana. E-38 was one of 84 units built by General Electric which entered service on 42 locomotives. Some of them were in service for 58 years. By 1950, E-38 was a combination of three "half-units." LEFT: Motor E-50 A, B and C lead train 266 through Missoula, Montana, on July 1, 1972. The Milwaukee Road used a 3,000-volt DC system that had evolved from General Electric's experience with the BA&P electrification. RIGHT: Switcher E-81 returned from Silver Bow, the connection with the Union Pacific, with a local just west of Butte, Montana, on June 30, 1972. Four switchers were built by General Electric. They served virtually their entire careers in Montana. *(Two photos FWS)*

The final years of The Milwaukee Road's electrification in Montana were personified by The Little Joes. Built by General Electric, 12 of these locomotives served from 1951 until electric service ended on June 15, 1974. FACING PAGE: On July 2, 1972, E-76 led train 261 at East Portal, Montana, the summit of the Bitterroot Mountains. *(FWS)* The Milwaukee Road acquired the 12 Little Joes for a lot price of $1,000,000, a bargain for a unit which could produce 5,100 continuous horsepower. The locomotives were originally built for service in Russia. Their long, fixed wheelbase was not designed for 10-degree curves and mountain grades; thus, they produced heavy flange and rail wear on The Milwaukee Road. ABOVE: On June 22, 1960, two Little Joes led this train which was descending the east slope of the mountains at Grace, Montana. OVERLEAF: Extra E-73 East, Train 264, passes Gold Creek, Montana, on July 29, 1960. This site of Milwaukee's last spike was between Garrison and Drummond, just 1-1/4 miles west of Northern Pacific's last spike site. In 1988, The Milwaukee Road and this track are history. The N.P. track is now part of The Montana Rail Link. *(Two photos Philip C. Johnson)*